The Death of
PROPAGANDA

B2B buyer behavior has changed – now it's your turn

Jonathan Winch   Michael Best   David Hoskin

Three Voices™strategy

ISBN 978-87-994949-0-3

First published in 2011 by
Eye for Image ApS
Bredgade 4, 2 tv
DK-1260 Copenhagen

www.eye-for-image.com

Royal Danish Library cataloging-in-publication data. A catalog record for this book is available from the Royal Danish Library.

Cover design and typesetting by Eye for Image.
Printed in Denmark.

CONTENTS

ACKNOWLEDGEMENTS

Many people have contributed their time, enthusiasm and expertise
to the creation of this book and to the development of the Three Voices™
strategic framework.

Early on, we recognized the strength and wisdom of crowd-sourcing,
and pre-released 500 review copies of this book, gathering feedback along
the way and making adjustments as appropriate. As a result, the book you now
hold in your hands or are reading on your screen draws not just on the authors'
knowledge and expertise but also on invaluable ideas and insights contributed
by many of our clients, business partners, peers and a wide range of others
(many of whom we have yet to meet in person). We'd like to express our
gratitude to all who have been willing to share their views as we explored why
propaganda must die and how the Three Voices™ can carry the load instead.

In addition, we'd particularly like to thank Thomas Webster, Jens Victor Fischer,
Michael Carney, Jomar Reyes, Michael Leander, Randy Morgan, Kathryn Casey and
Sine Finne Frandsen. Without the efforts of these people, we might have worked
our way through the project, but the result wouldn't have been anywhere
near as effective as the book we can now share with you.

Jonathan Winch
Michael Best
David Hoskin

Copenhagen, April 2012

ABOUT THE AUTHORS

Jonathan Winch is a partner and co-founder of Copenhagen-based advertising agency Eye for Image. A native of New Zealand, Jonathan has enjoyed a B2B-focused marketing and communication career spanning more than 25 years, making strategic contributions to businesses such as Johnson & Johnson, Nokia Siemens Networks, Cisco, LEGO and many other brands. Most recently, Jonathan's work has included Three Voices™-inspired projects for a number of internationally focused B2B companies, perhaps the most notable of which is DuPont Nutrition & Health.

David Hoskin, a partner in and co-founder of Eye for Image, and another New Zealand expatriate, has spent the past decade helping household-name Danish companies bring their products, ideas and passions to an international stage. An expert in B2B content creation, David is focused on the design and management of processes to support organizations seeking to implement Three Voices™ market strategies. David is a frequent speaker on aspects of international marketing and a guest lecturer at Denmark's Institute of Study Abroad.

Michael Best hails from Baltimore, Maryland. For the past 25 years, operating as an innovation consultant and creative director, Michael has developed a keen eye for the visual and customer experience design aspects of B2B sales and marketing strategies. His blend of creativity and strategic advisory skills has helped companies such as Avaya, Danaher Corporation, the U.S. Department of Defense, Milliken Carpet, and CellularOne. Moving to Copenhagen, and joining Eye for Image as a partner in January 2010, Michael has been integral to the continuous advancement of Three Voices™ principles and tools, with particular emphasis on Voice of Company and Voice of Industry platform design.

All three authors blog at ***www.integratedb2b.com***

FOREWORD

Why this book? Why now? On the one hand, we regularly hear the comment that there are too few books on business-to-business (B2B) business strategy, particularly in the field of marketing. But that's not what led us to start this project. In fact, the journey commenced many months before we decided to write this book—and it began with trying to solve a difficult problem we realized all of our B2B clients were facing.

For years, we've watched our clients struggling to get their minds (and budgets) around the principles and techniques of integrated marketing. And we've watched them attempt to put together communication plans that combine offline with online activities. Unfortunately, time after time they kept running into the same challenge.

That seemingly insurmountable problem? The lack of a cohesive strategic framework that encompasses B2B marketing in all of its aspects—starting with a single view of today's much-evolved B2B stakeholder, which leads in turn to tightly integrated communications efforts (whether online or offline is immaterial) that cater to this stakeholder's current and future needs. Without that holistic framework, B2B marketing is inevitably less than the sum of its parts.

Until we began the journey toward the realizations described in this book, our problem was this: for all our knowledge of how to work with offline and online marketing and communications, we hadn't really made the transition to a holistic framework either.

In years gone by, we created numerous PowerPoint presentations that laid out statistic after frightening statistic about the changes underway in the marketing landscape, before launching into descriptions of SEO/SEM, mobile marketing, behavioral targeting and so on. Mostly, our audiences seemed to understand what we were saying. They came away with a notion of urgency and a somewhat better understanding of the specific techniques of online marketing. What we have always felt was lacking, however, was an "Aha! experience"—that moment of revelation where the clouds evaporate and all becomes crystal clear.

An Aha! experience motivates like nothing else. It changes attitudes, creates direction, frees up resources and gets you on track for far better results. It gives you boxes in which to organize the various bits of knowledge so that you can better remember and work with your new level of understanding. What was needed was a strategic framework that delivered a powerful Aha! experience for our audiences.

With this aim in mind, we set out to create just such a framework, primarily as a tool for our clients and our colleagues. After hundreds of hours of interviews, desk research, discussions and more than a few complete re-thinks, our Aha! experience finally saw the light of day during an intense discussion late one Friday afternoon. We called the new framework "Three Voices™ strategy". And, a few months later, people began suggesting we put it all into a book. Which is exactly what we did.

Many of the ideas we present here are nothing new (we would be the first to admit that), drawing upon established practices in market research, branding, content marketing and organizational structuring. But the power of Three Voices™ strategy lies in its ability to bring it all together, providing clarity and structure to the rather confusing world of integrated marketing. To put it in the words of one executive from a leading global chemicals manufacturer, "It's not like we didn't know a lot of these things before, it's just that it never made collective sense—we never had a big picture that could help us to work strategically rather than tactically."

That's why, these days, we're urging the CEOs, marketing directors and communications vice presidents we meet to get their minds around this new framework and use it to convince their organizations of the need to significantly re-think and re-organize their market approaches.

We know Three Voices™ strategy is an idea that works. First, because it caused a major Aha! experience for ourselves and our colleagues. Then, because we've seen its effect on company after company. We've seen executives literally jump out of their chairs and walk excitedly around the room, energized by their new understanding and its implications for how they can reach and engage their B2B audiences. And we've been energized by it, too. It has enabled us to discover hidden opportunities and caused us to build new capabilities and platforms for both our agency and its clients.

At the same time, discovering our Aha! experience has made us keen to get the message out to as many people as possible as quickly as possible. And that's where this book comes in—to bring the Aha! experience of Three Voices™ strategy to many more people than those we've been able to help directly.

This book is the first step on your Three Voices™ journey. Once you're ready to move to the next stage, go to **www.threevoicesstrategy.com** and participate in or watch from the sidelines as the framework, its insights, tools and processes evolve.

Down with Propaganda!
Long live Credibility!

W hy do so many B2B corporations think that corporate speak is a valid way of talking to their customers (while at the same time ignoring similar nonsense from their own suppliers)?

Take a look at the messages below, taken from the corporate website of a technology provider:

- [Name] offers innovative solutions with unrivalled comprehensive functionality, flexible implementation and a truly global reach.

- [Name] has unmatched implementation success, excellent customer base, thousands of satisfied users.

- Secure your access to new functionality and technology while protecting your investment and lowering your cost of ownership.

What do you do when you see messages like these? Our guess is, you don't waste your precious time reading them. And you don't get warm, fuzzy feelings about the company trying so naively to win you over. Being a savvy buyer yourself, you know when someone is trying to sell to you. Superlatives, exaggeration, dubious claims and the like don't impress you. In fact, they're just as likely to cause you to reject the seller before they have a chance to explain the real value they can deliver.

Despite this, many otherwise intelligent, well-educated people in the management, marketing and communication departments of corporations continue to produce superlative-laden, clichéd statements delivered by the company from the company's own perspective.

Sadly, much of what passes for marketing in the B2B space can be thought of as propaganda, a term defined by the Oxford Dictionary as "information, especially of a biased or misleading nature, used to promote a political cause or point of view". Often, corporate propaganda is created to please upper management rather than the customers it seems to be addressing.

These days, propaganda doesn't work so well in marketing. In pre-Internet times there were significant limits to the ways in which information could be gathered by potential purchasers. In the B2B space, business magazines, trade shows and occasional books were seen as comparatively objective sources of knowledge about specialist products and services. Beyond those, would-be buyers seldom had anywhere else to turn for information except to those actually selling the products or services. Conflicting claims and counter-claims were commonplace as competing salespeople pitched their propaganda and prospects were forced to judge for themselves which assertions were the most credible.

Times have certainly changed. Now, intending purchasers have many methods of gathering information, well before they need to involve those who have a vested interest in any sale. For example, they can (and do) talk amongst themselves.

There's a conversation going on about you— without you

Your audiences are talking about you—in places that you know about, and in all sorts of forums to which you haven't been invited. Today's B2B buyers join or engage with a wide variety of subject-matter-specific forums and personal connections, both online and offline, to help them gather information and understand the challenges, opportunities and tools of their trade.

Increasingly, these either formally arranged or casual conversations are where the real action is, and where B2B companies need to focus their attention. Greatly enabled by the Internet and other technologies, this is where people are informing about, recommending or trashing brands with greater influence than any conventional, company-driven promotional efforts. Here, competitive battles are won or lost, often without a vendor even being a part of the conversation.

59% of B2B buyers researching a potential purchase spoke about it with peers who had considered a similar product or service

DemandGen Report *"Breaking Out Of The Funnel", 2010*

...

The conversations center around which types of solutions are most likely to prove effective, such as whether to place one's bets on one technological direction or another, and on which brands that can deliver the chosen solution should be placed on the prospective buyer's short list—or disregarded. Propaganda-fueled marketing messages and sales approaches don't improve the chances of getting your company's products or services on that short list. In fact, they may have quite the opposite effect.

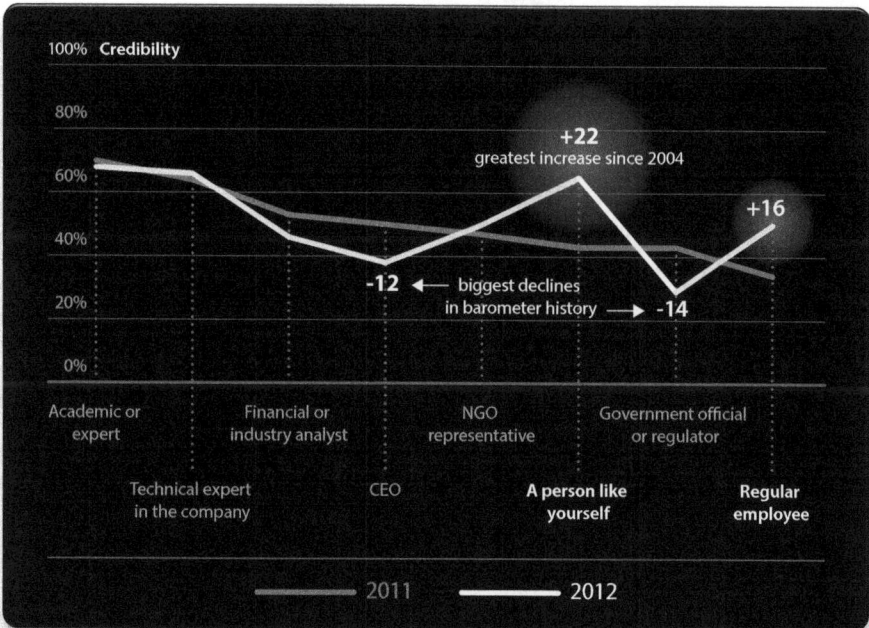

Figure i.1 The dramatic rise in the credibility of peers and regular employees according to the 2012 Edelmann Trust Barometer (http://trust.edelman.com/).

The more you sell, the less you sell

One of the biggest gaps between what today's new breed of B2B buyer wants and the way most B2B companies communicate can be summed up in one word: credibility.

That's what's missing, by and large, from those carefully crafted messages designed to persuade the masses using superlatives such as "advanced", "state-of-the-art", "cutting edge" and the like. Many meters of such copy have been painstakingly created over the years by and for all manner of businesses.

What a waste. Today's B2B buyers are increasingly sourcing the information they need from discussions on third-party sites, by asking questions on LinkedIn, reading user ratings and reviews, visiting blogs and so on. Visits to corporate websites are still highly relevant and often used by prospective buyers, but the credibility of the information gathered in this way is less well regarded than that of independent comments.

You might think that those who commission misguided promotional propaganda must surely be aware of the new reality. After all, they too live and work in this brave new world of peer-supported decision-making and are just as likely to reject inappropriate marketing materials aimed at themselves.

Faced with an increasingly skeptical audience, however, some marketers are reacting in a similar way to the Catholic Church when challenged by the Reformation during the mid-fifteenth century: instead of joining the ranks of those whose eyes had been gradually opened to a new, more down-to-earth paradigm, the church chose to spend even more money, creating ever more ornate, glitter-laden cathedrals in an effort to impress the masses into staying loyal. It was a desperate attempt to stick with the old business model. Needless to say, it's hard to stop progress—as the Church soon discovered.

Traditionally thinking marketers and communicators should apply lessons learned from the Reformation and Counter-Reformation to their situation today. The Marketing Reformation has a fast-increasing number of followers out there searching the Internet, practicing direct and honest peer-to-peer communications, primarily relying on the judgment of people like themselves rather than the propaganda disseminated by company websites and marketing collateral. Of course, for many at the corporate end, it's also likely to take something akin to religious fervor to change the fundamentals of their company's approach to its market!

If you plan to carry on feeding the propaganda machine, consider the likely business impact as phrased by *The NOW Revolution* co-author Jay Baer: "The key paradox of modern marketing is that the more you 'sell' the less you sell."

The need for a new approach

Given all these paradigm-shifting transformations, it's clear that B2B businesses need to develop a more carefully structured platform for engaging stakeholders. Describing this, and framing it in terms of three distinct "Voices" that make it easier to visualize and work with the task of creating such a platform, is the key purpose of this book.

The need for a new way of describing the way B2B companies should engage with their various stakeholders made itself painfully obvious in two common situations we encountered at our agency: first, when we discussed the principles and likely best practices of integrating online and offline marketing and communication among ourselves (which often resulted in heated discussions between "old world" and "new world" communicators); and second, when we attempted to explain these ideas to our B2B clients. The problem, it seemed, was the lack of a common, consistent language for talking about the many and varied aspects of marketing and communication today.

Those of us who were born and raised in an essentially offline world of advertising tend to think in a certain way and use a particular set of terms when talking about our work. We're focused on things like value propositions, storylines and visual identities. We know that simplicity and clarity are key elements behind powerful persuasion, and seek these essentials in everything we do. And, until recently, we've been perfectly comfortable producing and fine-tuning what we might now consider largely to be propaganda. The world of social media and other forms of online presence often seems complex and diffuse to us.

On the other hand, those of us whose career paths have favored online forms of communication are of a different persuasion. We're entirely comfortable with technology-driven approaches to marketing, get excited about getting people joined up into communities (often without a clear idea of why), have a lot of faith in the essential goodness of humankind, and disdain all forms of overtly persuasive marketing messages.

Many members of this latter group have long held the notion that traditional marketers are wrong and they themselves hold the truth in their digitally oriented grasp. That attitude, we believe, is changing fast. Today, there's a growing realization that both of these mindsets and skillsets are necessary to achieve lasting success for B2B companies. As yet, however, there are few people who are equally comfortable moving in both worlds. Traditional marketing types, both at agencies and their clients, have clung to what they know, incorporating online tools and activities sporadically rather than as part of their general approach.

On the digital side, the technical and pioneering nature of online approaches has meant that practitioners have tended to develop silo skills in, for example, the tools of mobile marketing or search engine optimization. Strangely enough, their solutions to client problems tend to recommend these particular tools, no matter what the issue at hand may actually demand. After all, if all you have is a hammer, as the saying goes, you treat everything as if it were a nail!

As we sought, over many months of exchanges and exploration both at our agency and with our clients, to find a better way to think about such things, the clouds began to clear and a common way of speaking about stakeholder engagement appeared (rather like a sequel to the Tower of Babel). The new framework, which we call Three Voices™ Strategy, seemed to make perfect sense—to us and also to the marketing and communications professionals to whom we presented it. See if you agree.

Today's B2B businesses must speak in many tongues

A Three Voices™ strategy, in essence, is a stakeholder engagement model that stretches across all of a company's audiences. It rests on three concepts that are vital for B2B marketers and communicators to grasp: Voice of Company, Voice of Industry, and Voice of Customer.

The basic idea of a Three Voices™ strategy is easily described on a paper napkin in less than ten minutes. That's because the principles underlying it are relatively simple and can be communicated by drawing three circles, each representing one of the Voices as shown in Figure i.2.

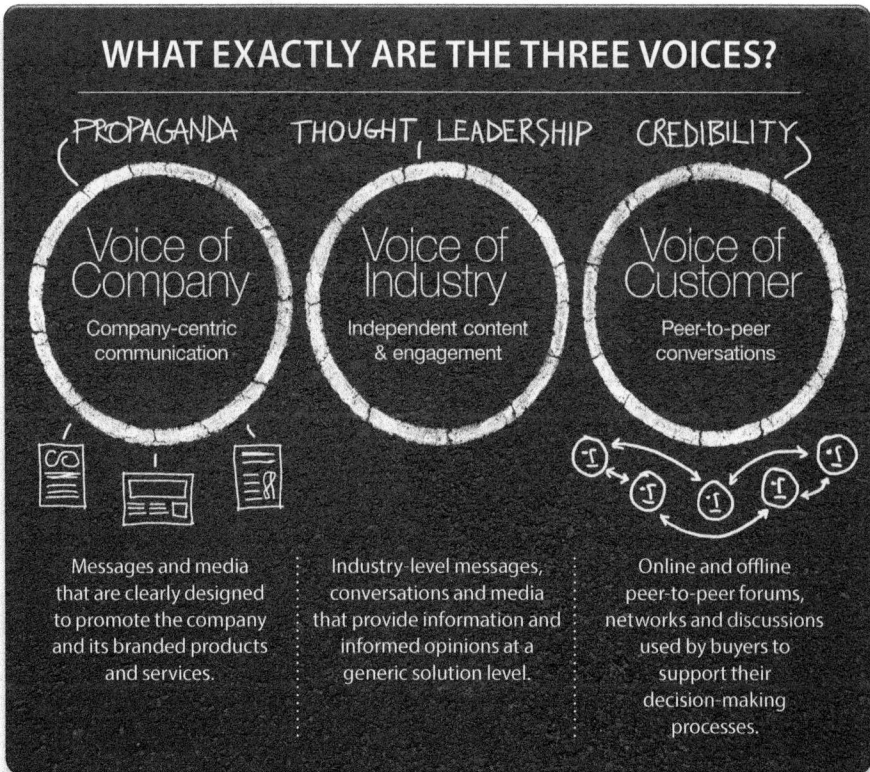

WHAT EXACTLY ARE THE THREE VOICES?

PROPAGANDA   THOUGHT LEADERSHIP   CREDIBILITY

| Voice of Company | Voice of Industry | Voice of Customer |
| Company-centric communication | Independent content & engagement | Peer-to-peer conversations |

| Messages and media that are clearly designed to promote the company and its branded products and services. | Industry-level messages, conversations and media that provide information and informed opinions at a generic solution level. | Online and offline peer-to-peer forums, networks and discussions used by buyers to support their decision-making processes. |

Figure i.2 An overview of the Three Voices™ framework.

Voice of Company

Let's begin with the circle on the left, representing the Voice of Company. We use Voice of Company as an umbrella term for messages and materials created by a manufacturer or service provider to describe its offerings to prospective customers. Specifically, we're talking about ads, brochures, data sheets, trade show stands, the corporate website and so on—any piece of communication where the company is providing brand-centric information with itself strongly established as the communicator.

Essentially, Voice of Company describes what most companies are doing today—communicating messages about products, services, events and so on from the standpoint of the company. When B2B buyers encounter these messages on a website or in corporate marketing materials, they are entirely aware that these messages have been crafted by the company itself. So the viewer of such messages is at once on guard—wary of being manipulated by someone who so clearly wants to make a sale, do a deal or make some profit. It's like a mousetrap with the mouse gingerly circling the cheese, expecting at any moment to be crushed by the snap of a deadly wire.

These days, however, buyers have found a way around the polished promotions produced by most B2B companies. Often, before they've ever encountered your official messages, and before deciding whether or not to include you on their shortlist, they have used the internet as well as offline forums to gain an impression of your company's offerings.

If all your Voice of Company materials then do is to paint a glowing picture of perfection (to people who have already discovered a few home truths about your brand), you just might be telling prospective customers that you are either ignorant of what the market truly thinks or you've just decided to ignore it!

In today's world of B2B marketing and communications, Voice of Company is undeniably the home of corporate propaganda. And it's where most B2B marketing resources are focused, with the company seeking to convince prospective buyers that its products are best by directly telling them so.

The key strategic direction in this arena, as far as a Three Voices™ strategy is concerned, should be to *reduce or eliminate propaganda-like messages* and become a more credible entity that is seen to help prospects and customers to determine the solution that best fits their needs.

Of course, Voice of Company has its rightful place in the new world of B2B evaluation and purchasing. Here's where the company can provide useful information that explains the product's features and benefits, specifications and SKU codes in order to encourage and facilitate purchasing. B2B buyers like (and need) to be able to access such information. And here is also where you can provide another entry point to your company's industry-level content, campaigns and communities. But that's pretty much where it stops. For sophisticated, and increasingly skeptical audiences, the rest of the verbal and visual decoration is now mostly propaganda. And this evolution is exactly where the other two Voices find their reason for existence.

Voice of Customer

Now let's turn our attention to the circle on the right called Voice of Customer. We use this term to describe the peer-to-peer conversations going on between B2B buyers, discussing and recommending—or warning against—specific solutions and products, often well before any manufacturers are consulted. These peer-to-peer exchanges, via independent or largely independent online and offline discussion forums, carry the highest level of believability and trustworthiness that can be achieved in today's mass communication environments.

Here's where all the action is, where the big changes in B2B buyer behavior have taken place, where short lists are determined, and where companies need to actively *listen and respond* if they are to match their marketing efforts to the new realities of B2B buying processes.

Historically, "Voice of the Customer" (VOC) has been a term used to describe targeted programs for involving customers in core corporate activities such as product development and the design of customer-facing functions. Today, however, we hear from our clients that this concept is fast becoming outdated, its practices have become too costly and its outcomes inaccurate and insufficient. In fact, such programs have been a stop-gap measure that was only ever useful as a far-too-small plaster on a gaping wound in the way businesses were interacting with their customers. Enlightened B2B marketers now look past traditional Voice of the Customer programs to get customer input on the customer's terms rather than those of the company.

Voice of Industry

If Voice of Company is where most B2B companies focus their activities today, and Voice of Customer is where the real action takes place, then the middle arena, Voice of Industry, should be seen as the bridge companies need to use to close the gap. By Voice of Industry we mean activities where the company seeks to influence its market and enhance its brand by discussing industry-level matters instead of directly pushing its own offerings.

This Voice is already a well-established part of the new breed of B2B buyer's information-gathering practices. Excellent (online) examples are to be found in the myriad of industry-specific or technology-specific websites out there today. Customers and prospects tap into sites such as Food Navigator, Baking Business or TechCrunch, reading the information they present and/or checking regular newsletters or bulletins as they arrive via channels such as email or Twitter. Here they gain access to information that, while it may have been initiated by a company, a somewhat biased trade journalist or an analyst keen on getting his or her name in lights, has a greater degree of credibility than a company website where everything is aimed at selling products and services.

Traditionally, the publisher of such generalist industry information has not been a manufacturer, but an information-oriented party such as a magazine publisher, a research company, a buyer's guide publisher, an academic institution or similar; or perhaps a well-regarded industry professional. Many of these sources do have a product or service to sell, but give these a back seat, sharing their subject knowledge with others as a subtle way of promoting their wares. Others share their knowledge to build their personal brands, out of altruistic motives or from sheer enthusiasm for the subject matter.

The opportunity for B2B businesses lies in the extra *credibility* (yes, the special ingredient missing from propaganda) earned by representing the industry rather than purely the interests of a specific company—and by becoming an industry advocate instead of a salesperson. Of course, we would never recommend doing this in an underhand, stealthy fashion. Companies working within Voice of Industry contexts must always make their efforts transparent, albeit in an understated way in comparison with the strong branding of their Voice of Company activities.

Typically, Voice of Industry activities encompass paid media (paying to place industry-level content on other companies' media), earned media (being seen as a valuable content partner on, for example, an independent industry news site, or setting up and feeding content to a company-branded LinkedIn group), and the all-important owned media (you own and control a content platform that prospects and customers use to help them make buying decisions).

One example of an owned-media Voice of Industry activity is Adobe, Inc.'s CMO.com. Branded discretely with a small Adobe logo in the top right corner, the site offers "digital marketing insight for chief marketing officers", including news items, trend articles, marketing analytics, reports, surveys, statistics and commentary from industry experts—along with other digital marketing resources that have a relatively long shelf life.

In our view (and following the logic of a Three Voices™ strategy), Adobe's investment in CMO.com is most likely designed to engage marketing management at an industry or solution level, developing a base of registered subscribers and creating a valuable communications channel for marketing purposes. Adobe's interest in this particular audience is, no doubt, driven by the company's product portfolio, which includes one of the marketing automation industry's most advanced and comprehensive systems. The investment required for such a system requires CMO sign-off—thus the need to engage with, educate and build relationships with CMOs.

Adobe's provision of useful, meaningful information to CMOs via its Voice of Industry site is likely to enhance the company's status among its customers as a value-adding business partner rather than as just another vendor trying to push its products.

And here lies one of the single most important points of this book:

> The ultimate goal of a properly implemented Three Voices™ strategy is to move from the company telling prospects and customers "We're great!" to having those audiences telling each other "They're great!"

To reach that exalted status, companies need to build effective Voice of Industry activities, move from propaganda to credibility, and shift from being traditional salespeople to the role of customer advocates.

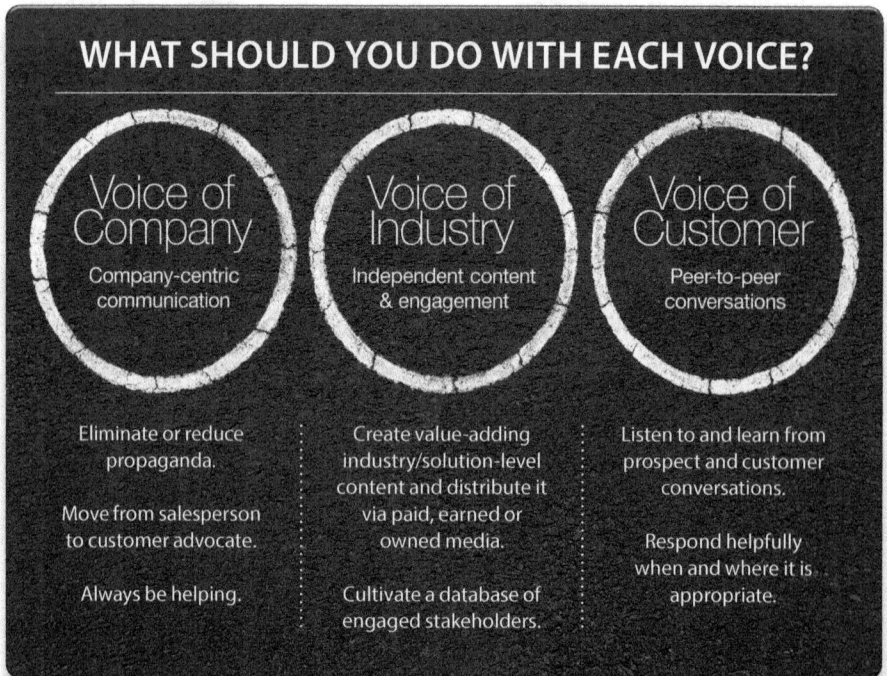

WHAT SHOULD YOU DO WITH EACH VOICE?

Voice of Company	Voice of Industry	Voice of Customer
Company-centric communication	Independent content & engagement	Peer-to-peer conversations
Eliminate or reduce propaganda.	Create value-adding industry/solution-level content and distribute it via paid, earned or owned media.	Listen to and learn from prospect and customer conversations.
Move from salesperson to customer advocate.		Respond helpfully when and where it is appropriate.
Always be helping.	Cultivate a database of engaged stakeholders.	

Figure i.3 The task for each Voice in the Three Voices™ framework.

Is a Three Voices™ strategy just another way of saying "social media strategy"?

When it comes to the online expression of your Three Voices™ strategy, social media (which is a term that usually refers to online social networking) can be a key component. But a Three Voices™ strategy encompasses both online and offline forms of marketing and communication. And the interplay between these is important.

In this book therefore, a "social network" refers to any gathering point where groups of people meet and mingle—on a website, at a cocktail party, during an industry conference—anywhere they can form lasting relationships with a particular, themed group that has an established means of communication between its members, and where the aim of the members is primarily to connect to and share with other members.

Can there be overlap between different Voices?

As we were developing the Three Voices™ framework, we quickly noticed that it wasn't always possible to describe the activities of some companies as clearly either Voice of Company or Voice of Industry. The distinction will always be an arbitrary one, but one key question can help to shed light on the choice of description:

> "To what extent does the audience perceive that
> it is being sold to or being helped?"

If your intention is to have your company perceived as an industry-level thought leader (which we would most definitely advocate for most B2B organizations), then you should work as objectively with the Voice of Industry context as possible. That means, for example, choosing a neutral environment for your Voice of Industry communications and avoiding the temptation to deliver those industry-level messages via your heavily branded corporate website.

For many companies embarking on a Three Voices™ strategy, however, early attempts to create a Voice of Industry platform are likely to be overly influenced by the company's brand. After all, it's hard to change deeply entrenched marketing habits overnight. In particular, many B2B companies will initially find it difficult to bring the opinions of outside experts into their Voice of Industry activities—a key component of achieving a high level of credibility. Our advice is to make the leap as far as you can, creating a Voice of Industry that is as far from your Voice of Company activities as possible rather than landing on a compromise that leaves your audiences feeling they are, in fact, just experiencing a slightly more creative version of your normal corporate marketing activities.

Three Voices™ strategy and thought leadership

In our opinion, while its principles provide useful insights for companies of all kinds, a Three Voices™ approach is strongly suited to knowledge-intensive companies—in particular, those whose key audiences are closely involved with the company's product or service specialty. If we refer back to the earlier example of Adobe Inc.'s Voice of Industry site CMO.com, Adobe's audience is likely to be highly interested (or should be!) in methods of optimizing their marketing activities via information systems. So, at least in theory, it should not be especially difficult to get decision-makers, particularly those in larger companies who can afford Adobe's marketing automation system, regularly involved with the subject matter.

More and more, knowledge-intensive companies are beginning to talk about a comparatively new competitive parameter—at least in a marketing rather than a product delivery context. "Thought leadership" is business jargon for an entity that is recognized for having innovative ideas or interesting new perspectives and for communicating them. The term is said to have been coined in 1994 by Joel Kurtzman, editor-in-chief of the Booz Allen Hamilton magazine, Strategy & Business, but hasn't been widely used in B2B contexts beyond the publications of professional consulting firms. And it seems there's money in it, too. IBM believes so strongly in the benefits of thought leadership that it established the Institute for Business Value (IBV), comprised of more than 50 consultants who conduct research and analysis across multiple industries and functional disciplines. In our own industry, we've noticed IBV publications such as its Global CMO Study turning up on the desks of business executives and being widely referenced in online Voice of Customer and Voice of Industry contexts, proving perhaps, that high-quality, credible content reaches far indeed.

We believe that thought leadership lies at the heart of a Three Voices™ strategy for knowledge-intensive companies, and that Voice of Industry activities are the prime vehicle for promoting your company as a thought leader. We're also fascinated by the idea that, for many knowledge-intensive companies, the way in which B2B buyers now evaluate solutions and brands opens up an opportunity to bring the company's brand much closer to its essential DNA.

An example may serve to clarify the point: that of Danisco A/S, a large Danish-based manufacturer of food ingredients that was acquired by DuPont in 2011 and now is part of DuPont Nutrition & Health. According to Danisco's management—and confirmed by a recent customer survey—one of the key reasons behind the company's successful track record of growth and profitability over the years has been the attitude and skills of its people. That may sound like propaganda, but it does, in fact, seem that the hundreds of scientists and application experts working closely with the company's customers to solve problems, devise new recipes, and refine existing formulae have delivered a high-quality customer experience that has built Danisco's business.

In any case, the success cannot be attributed to a powerful marketing machine since, somewhat like its new parent company, Danisco was never particularly focused on telling the industry how good it was, preferring to place its bets on science, application knowledge and what its customers have described as "approachability". That's the type of highly desirable reputation that is usually trumpeted in flamboyant corporate claims—except that making such claims hasn't been Danisco's style. Like many knowledge-intensive companies, especially the scientifically based variety, people are cautious about overstating capabilities—even too cautious.

Branding a company like the former Danisco, then, isn't a matter of sending in an Armani-suited, glass-officed team of advertising agency front men who pay lip service to the company's essential way of being, then charge the earth to create a highly polished store window with little connection to reality. Instead, it's more about exposing and highlighting the expertise, opinions, and passions of the previously unsung heroes within the company—bringing the organization's true expertise to a much larger audience around the globe. We call the creation of this new asset "scaleable DNA", leveraging a Three Voices™ strategy to magnify a company's natural strengths.

Does it mean you have to tell the truth?

In this new world of straight-up, transparent, credible interactions with the company's audiences, the truth is playing an increasingly important role. The trend is driven partly by the fact that attitudes are hardening toward corporate lies or other malpractices—just witness the number of whistle-blower programs that are being implemented across industries to enable employees to keep their employers and colleagues on the straight and narrow. In marketing contexts, easier access to essential truths about products and services—true stories shared by real customers—means that propaganda and/or outright fibs stand out like a sore thumb.

During a presentation of our thoughts to a group of representatives from mid-sized B2B companies, one executive asked an excellent question: "What if telling the truth about your company would mean telling the market that, in actual fact, your products weren't that good, that they failed often, that they were over-priced?"

It may seem harsh, but today's business environment means that there should be little or no disconnect between your company's delivered competencies and offerings and the picture you paint for the outside world. Companies that provide sub-standard products and services (where significant cover-up is a way of life) need to revamp what they're doing before they can expect to succeed over the long term in today's increasingly transparent marketplaces.

In other words, if your company falls into this unfortunate category, then a properly implemented Three Voices™ strategy is most likely not for you. Not yet. But don't stop reading, because if you've gotten this far, we expect that you are planning to change things for the better one way or another.

Start with the customer

We've already thoroughly canvassed the issue of propaganda and why it's no longer relevant in a B2B environment. However, there's a whole lot more to a Three Voices™ strategy than simply displacing traditional propaganda with new, improved versions of your messages.

Marketers tend to talk about "the B2B buyer" as if he or she were a single individual tasked with making decisions on behalf of the organization (and given carte blanche to do so). The reality, however, is substantially more complicated. The audience whose collective opinion you might seek to sway is (in all but the smallest of organizations) a group of people with different perspectives and requirements.

Who they are, and the most important issues that must be resolved if you are to have any hope of selling them on your solution, is the focus of chapter one.

Key take-outs

- Three Voices™ Strategy is a new framework for understanding and closing the gap between the way today's B2B companies try to attract customers and the fast-changing behavior of B2B buyers.

- Businesses are still churning out self-congratulatory propaganda rather than engaging in useful or meaningful communications.

- Propaganda pleases the company's management, not its customers.

- Propaganda doesn't have the effect it once had, in today's B2B marketplace (the more you sell, the less you sell!).

- Now buyers talk among themselves and consult industry-level sources as the primary drivers of purchasing decisions—without you.

- 59% of B2B buyers researching a potential purchase spoke about it with peers who had considered a similar product or service.

- Companies need to move from propaganda to credibility—and a Three Voices™ strategy facilitates this move.

- "Always be helping" is the new "Always be closing".

- A key goal is to move from the company telling prospective buyers how good it is to a new situation where *buyers* tell their peers how good the company is.

- A Three Voices™ strategy is particularly suited to knowledge-intensive companies with highly involved audiences.

Questions for B2B strategists

- Has your company moved with the times or is it still working with the old sales and marketing paradigm?

- Does your company website use words like "advanced", "leading" and other propaganda-like superlatives? Does it communicate from the customer's point of view or from its own?

- To what degree do buyers considering products like yours consult their peers for advice? Are they active in discussion forums in which you don't or can't participate?

- What would happen if your company told the "truth" about its products and services? Would there be a disconnect between the story your marketing materials communicate and the real customer experience?

Notes

CHAPTER ONE

The new breed of B2B buyer

Just three out of a hundred B2B sales came from cold-calling

We've already discussed the new reality that your marketing and its propaganda-style messaging may not be working so well any more. You may also be finding that your organization's sales calls aren't delivering either.

A 2010 DemandGen Report survey asked B2B buyers in a variety of vertical industries (from software and technology to healthcare and financial services) about the first point of contact with the organization that eventually made the sale. The survey found that just three percent of those sales came from an initial cold call from the seller.

So what led to the other 97 percent of sales?

- 33% of successful sales contacts were originated directly by the buyer.

- 53% came from the sales force following up after the buyer requested more information from the seller's website.

- 11% happened as a result of the buyer chatting with the seller through the website's live chat facility.

Those results are a staggering demonstration of the new reality: the buyer is totally in control, checking out products, sourcing peer reviews and choosing a (very) short list often before the seller has any idea that there's a possible sale in the wind.

Scary? You bet. Exhilarating and rich with possibilities if you can influence the buyer far earlier in the decision-making process? Absolutely.

The real action happens well before first contact

Google calls this whole before-the-sale process the *"Zero Moment of Truth"* and spells out the various elements from a consumer products perspective in an introductory video on the topic.

For our purposes, we've adapted the Zero Moment of Truth (ZMOT) thinking to the B2B space. Here's how the process might go:

1. The B2B prospect is motivated to consider making a purchase by some stimulus—it might be the need to replace worn-out equipment, an end-of-fiscal "use it or lose it" budget issue or simply a news item or even a piece of old-style marketing propaganda that inspires the buyer at the right time.

2. As a result of that stimulus, the prospect moves into active pre-shopping mode—"what should I buy?" Once upon a time, that pre-shopping mode might have involved calling in favored suppliers, issuing RFPs or looking up the specs in product catalogs or trade magazines. Nowadays, the internet is nearly always involved in this multistage process that Google called ZMOT. First comes search, as prospects start to browse through the possible options, fine-tuning their requirements and developing an understanding of exactly what types of products or services might suit their newly-diagnosed requirements. Typically, searches at this high level will involve broad descriptions of the customer need rather than detailed specifications of possible products or suppliers.

3. Once our prospect has identified avenues of enquiry that seem promising, the next step is to search for more detailed resource materials such as videos, reviews, white papers, articles and blog posts. The prospect's objective at this point is to conduct a deeper analysis of categories that at first glance seem they might fulfill the prospect's need.

4. In due course, the prospect (usually in consultation with colleagues) will decide on the most appropriate category to fit the need. Only then will the prospect's attention turn to the most suitable products within that category. At this point, the prospect will begin to search for specific types of product or service (though not yet for brands).

5. Once a preliminary selection of product/service types has been made, prospects nowadays typically look to their peers for recommendations, talking to well-informed colleagues in their own networks and searching out product reviews to reinforce or discard their own selections.

6. At around this point, prospects will finally make their first visits to seller websites. Most of the key decisions have already been made; information gathered from seller sites is typically for validation and reinforcement only.

7. Once the ideal options have been identified through the ZMOT process, the prospect moves into Buying Mode—"I know what I want, now where can I find the best deal?" This is when the would-be buyer first makes contact with the seller (sometimes anonymously)—far, far too late in the decision-making process for most sellers to be in a position to influence the purchase in ways other than price or service criteria.

This may seem like a doom and gloom scenario—and it is, for B2B marketing dinosaurs who haven't noticed the meteor shower. Fortunately, it's also the ideal opportunity to utilize a Three Voices™ strategy to interact with and influence the prospect—long before he or she comes into contact with any competitor.

Let's revisit the seven steps above, this time armed with our three Voices:

1. The B2B prospect is motivated to consider making a purchase by some Stimulus. That may be one of our marketing messages or even one of our competitors'—either is fine, if it starts the prospect on the ZMOT process.

2. The prospect moves into active pre-shopping mode via the Internet. He searches by broad descriptions. That's great—we're already there, well represented with rich Voice of Industry content that will be visible if his search touches any needs that our products or services meet (we optimize our titles, keywords and content based on needs and benefits, not product features).

3. Our prospect searches videos, reviews, white papers, articles and blog posts. We supply Voice of Industry content in those and many other formats.

4. The prospect begins to search for specific types of products or services. There's a very good chance he'll start to encounter our Voice of Company content—especially because he's now becoming more familiar with us through our Voice of Industry materials, and are more likely to engage with brands and organizations he recognizes.

5. Now the prospect turns to colleagues both online and offline. Here, thanks to our Voice of Customer initiatives, he'll hear from people with whom we're in regular contact—and, if we've been doing our job properly, those people will speak well of our organization and our products.

6. Next, prospects will go visiting websites. If our products truly do meet their needs, we're confident we'll be on that list.

7. Now the prospect calls us. We've already helped shape his thinking through our Voice of Industry materials, so the specifications should be a good match for what he's seeking. We expect to receive a fair hearing and have a solid chance of competing successfully for the business.

Even if the preceding description is a scenario that won't apply to all B2B buying processes, its principles should be taken as a clear warning of things to come.

Whatever happened to the Good Old Days?

In days gone by, the company's salespeople would typically be involved with the buying process from beginning to end. That made them an indispensable conduit and the main source of information about the company and its products. Salespeople also knew where the prospective buyer was in the process at any time—and were able to directly influence the direction and progress of each deal.

But things have changed. As we've seen in our ZMOT example above, the B2B prospect may not be in touch with sales representatives at all prior to the actual purchase—and even then, in some cases, everything may happen within the company's online environment instead of via personal contact. So prospects can find your offering, learn about it, see what others think of it, maybe even trial it and buy it, all without a salesperson. This new breed of B2B buyers gets its information from a wide variety of sources, including independent reviews, peer recommendations and content or community sites specific to the industry.

Let's look at some of the numbers (as you'll see, they support and reinforce the ZMOT scenario):

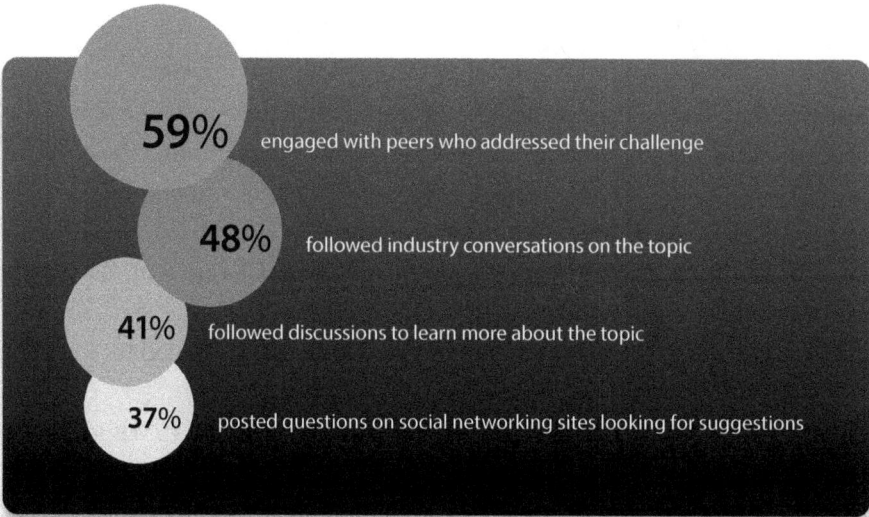

59% engaged with peers who addressed their challenge

48% followed industry conversations on the topic

41% followed discussions to learn more about the topic

37% posted questions on social networking sites looking for suggestions

Source: Genius.com/DemandGen Report White Paper, 2010:
"Breaking Out Of The Funnel - A Look Inside the Mind of the New Generation of BtoB Buyer"

Figure 1.1 How buyers researched potential purchases amongst their peers.
(Voice of Customer opportunities)

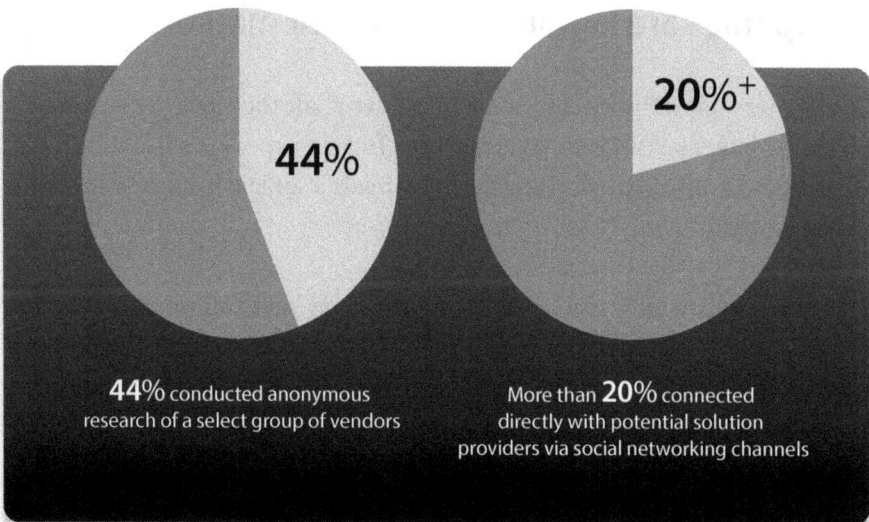

44% conducted anonymous research of a select group of vendors

More than **20%** connected directly with potential solution providers via social networking channels

Source: Genius.com/DemandGen Report White Paper, 2010:
"Breaking Out Of The Funnel - A Look Inside the Mind of the New Generation of BtoB Buyer"

Figure 1.2 Finally making contact. (Voice of Company opportunities)

Today's B2B buyer is more elusive than ever. And better informed. And more independent. So the playing field for marketers has become more of a battle field—battling for attention that is being given out at a premium. The problem is compounded by the level of "noise" encountered by consumers and business audiences alike. According to numbers presented in 2011 by Go-Globe, every 60 seconds around the world more than 160 million emails are sent, 12,000 ads are posted on Craigslist and 98,000 tweets are sent. In that same sixty seconds of every hour of every day, 48 hours of new videos are uploaded to YouTube.

Research published in January 2011 by B2B research provider ITSMA indicated that while buyers are avoiding salespeople in the early stages of the buying process—opting instead to spend their time with search, industry influencers, their peers, and social media—they still demand strong relationships with their suppliers. How can your company provide that relationship with its prospects and customers? That's a question that lies at the heart of this book and will be addressed in the chapters that follow.

Companies are lagging behind their markets

To date, very few B2B-oriented companies have made the move to keep up with changing buyer behavior in their markets. In fact, experience has shown that it's extremely difficult to find any that have made a sufficient effort to adopt the new paradigm.

The problem is widespread. Surprising as it may seem, almost none of the more than 100 companies with which we're in regular contact can point to a significant change in their marketing activities during the past five years. The vast majority are continuing the practices of the past decade or more in their attempts to reach and persuade business buyers.

B2B marketers need to make fundamental changes in the way they reach and persuade their audiences, given the undisputable shift in B2B buying behavior facilitated by the Internet. The current pace of change, however, is far too slow.

But why aren't B2B marketers quickly making the necessary changes? Don't they know what's going on? Are there too few resources in these times of economic instability? Or is it perhaps a lack of professionalism? While such factors may play a part, the real problem may be much more challenging: the sheer difficulty of understanding what is now required to effectively address the needs of the new breed of B2B buyers.

To come to terms with that challenge, as we'll see in the next chapter, we need to begin with a much deeper understanding of the customer.

Key take-outs

- These days, only a small percentage of B2B sales come from cold-calling.

- 78% of buyers start with informal information gathering.

- Buyers often gather enough information to make a decision before first contact with the company.

- The sales force has lost control of the customer's buying process.

- Few B2B businesses have changed their sales and marketing to fit buyers' new decision-making processes.

Questions for B2B strategists

- How do buyers gather information when considering products or services in your industry?

- At what point in the buying process do prospective buyers turn to your company? What do they already know and where or from whom might they have learned it?

- Has your company changed its sales and marketing approach and processes to match the changes in B2B buyer behavior?

- Is your marketing department still focused on creating "attractive" brochures and taglines rather than addressing the decision-making needs of buyers?

- What role do your salespeople play? Are they providing real value to buyers or just pushing your products?

Notes

Voice of
Customer

Peer-to-peer
conversations

Voice of Customer: Vendor-independent online and offline conversations taking place among people who want to learn about solutions to their challenges and build a shortlist of brands for closer evaluation.

CHAPTER TWO:

Voice of Customer

As we noted in the Introduction, customers are talking amongst themselves. And it's making all the difference to B2B marketing strategies going forward. But how exactly are they talking? Here are some typical examples from a study conducted amongst B2B buyers in the IT sector:

YOUR BUYERS ARE NOT ONLY FOLLOWING CONVERSATIONS, BUT ARE INITIATING DIALOGUE

71%	Follow discussions/conversations to learn more on public social networks and forums
67%	Post questions on public social networks and forums
66%	Connect with peers and thought leaders via social networking to set up private conversations
65%	Follow discussions/conversations to learn more on private, invite-only networks such as industry forums or vendor-sponsored communities
55%	Post questions on private invitation-only social networking sites (as above) for suggestions/feedback on how others solved challenges
51%	Connect directly with potential providers via social networking channels

Source: ITSMA and PAC, How Customers Choose Study, 2010

Figure 2.1 The use of social media during the IT solutions purchasing process.

If we intend to improve engagement with our prospective customers, and our ability to meet their needs, then we first need to understand more about who they are and what their roles are within their organizations.

Typically, for all but the smallest of B2B sales, there are a number of roles within a given organization that impact on the decision-making process. Figuring out different ways to describe these roles, particularly in relation to sales force strategies and tactics, has kept academics and practitioners busy for decades. Suffice to say, there are many ways to slice the cake, but for our purposes, we'll split the roles into five key categories:

1. **The User**: the person with the ultimate need for the product.

2. **The Influencer**: the person within the organization who understands the technical or strategic requirements of a given purchase and may shape the final specifications.

3. **The Purchaser**: this is the person, often a purchasing officer or a Chief Financial Officer, whose authorization is required to secure payment.

4. **The Decision-maker**: usually a CEO or senior executive, often makes a Yes/No decision based on the evidence presented to him or her in support of the purchase.

5. **The Gatekeeper**: typically a lower-level role, usually tasked with protecting the others from unwanted sales approaches; occasionally gathers information on behalf of others.

In any B2B purchasing process, the five roles tend to overlap:

	USER	INFLUENCER	PURCHASER	DECISION-MAKER	GATEKEEPER
(a) Identification of need	●	●			
(b) Establishing specifications & planning the purchase	●	●	●	●	
(c) Identifying buying alternatives	●	●	●		●
(d) Crowd-sourcing reviews & advice	●	●	●		
(e) Selecting the suppliers	●	●	●	●	

Adapted [except for (d)] from: Frederick E. Webster Jr. and Yoram Wind,
Organizational Buying Behavior, Prentice-Hall 1972

Figure 2.2 The five roles in B2B purchasing processes.

There are perhaps two significant changes to the classic model we've just described that have developed with the rise of pre-shopping via the Internet:

1. The **Gatekeeper** is somewhat less likely to be involved in information-gathering beyond the initial stages (unless he or she is particularly skilled in online search techniques).

2. **Crowd-sourcing**, as embodied in the addition of (d) to the model, has become the way that B2B buyers do due diligence online. To quote Gord Hotchkiss, CEO of Enquiro (The BuyerSphere Project, 2009): "If we don't have personal experience with a vendor, or know someone who does, we generally trust in the wisdom of crowds. This is the advantage the market leader has over the competition and the rationale embodied in the well-known quote, 'Nobody ever got fired for buying IBM.' If we choose the market leader and the decision goes badly, at least we can fall back on the claim that we had a lot of company."

In the purchasing model above, you'll recognize echoes of the Zero Moment of Truth process we discussed earlier. Our communications tasks do become more complicated with the realization that we actually need to take into account the needs of more than one type of B2B buyer—but it's a valuable reminder that we will need to provide information that prospective buyers can use to support their case to the final decision-makers anyway.

What information are prospects actually looking for?

The type of information sought by prospective purchasers depends very much on exactly where they are in the purchasing process. When they first start out on their journey, they're very much in exploratory mode; so general news and insights are most helpful. As prospects move beyond the background materials and are considering possible alternative solutions, their need is for more specific details and comparisons between possible solutions.

As they move closer to finalizing their selection, would-be purchasers will be keen to understand how their peers and others rate the possible alternatives (more about this shortly). Finally, once they've refined their selection criteria, these almost-buyers will gather information on specific suppliers and elicit credentials and pricing information.

The following table summarizes the process and indicates the sorts of information that prospects will find most useful at each step along the way:

Purchasing Process:	(b) Establishing specifications and planning the purchase	(c) Identifying buying alternatives	(e) Selecting the suppliers
Prospects Want:	Education and thought leadership	Solutions & product suitability	Credentials and decision support
What to Share:	Trends and statistics News and analyst coverage Benchmarks 101 education Ideas and inspiration Industry perspectives	Need and gap assessments Solution comparisons Implementation plans Product roadmaps	Credentials Real case-use studies Return On Investment Total Cost of Ownership How to build the business case How to buy
Voice Employed:	Voice of Industry	Voice of Industry and Voice of Company	Voice of Company

Adapted from presentation by BrainRider.com: "What Your Customer Wants To Know", March 2011

Figure 2.3 Useful information in the buying process.

Conspicuous by its absence from the above table is of course *Process (d)*, *Crowd-sourcing*—but we have only omitted it above so that we can discuss it in greater detail below.

Wisdom of the crowd

We've already noted the importance of peer opinions and reviews in the B2B consideration process. A recent study confirms that viewpoint (and in fact elevates such discussions to become the single most helpful part of the process):

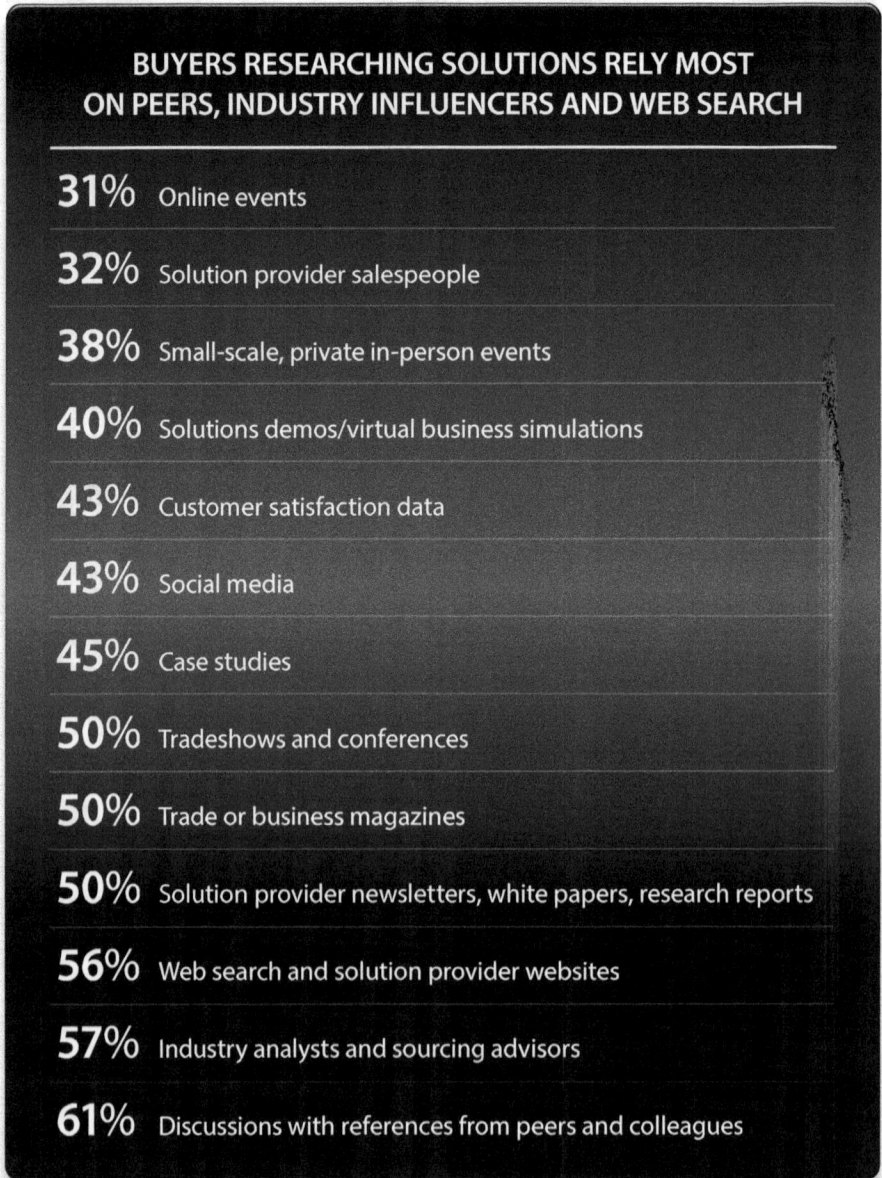

BUYERS RESEARCHING SOLUTIONS RELY MOST ON PEERS, INDUSTRY INFLUENCERS AND WEB SEARCH

31% Online events

32% Solution provider salespeople

38% Small-scale, private in-person events

40% Solutions demos/virtual business simulations

43% Customer satisfaction data

43% Social media

45% Case studies

50% Tradeshows and conferences

50% Trade or business magazines

50% Solution provider newsletters, white papers, research reports

56% Web search and solution provider websites

57% Industry analysts and sourcing advisors

61% Discussions with references from peers and colleagues

Source: ITSMA and PAC, How Customers Choose Study, 2010

Figure 2.4 Sources of information considered most helpful.

You'll notice from the chart that "solution provider salespeople" aren't a top priority—and regarded as helpful by less than a third of those B2B buyers polled. So how can vendors become part of the Voice of Customer discussion without being ignored at best, actively boycotted at worst?

Joining the conversation

To understand how you should behave in this new environment, consider the analogy of a cocktail party. Everyone stands around, gathered in small groups where they conduct more or less casual conversations. Those who have something interesting to say, are good at telling stories, or are known and respected for their achievements are typically the center of attention.

Now imagine that you (personifying your company) enter the room, unfashionably late. You edge up to one of the small groups, drink in hand, wearing a carefully tailored suit that loudly proclaims your corporate identity. Without listening first to hear what those already in the group are discussing, you begin proclaiming your excellence. Phrases such as "cutting edge", "high quality", "state-of-the-art" and "unique" pepper your monologue. What do you think the reactions of the others would be? Would they stand listening to you in admiration? Would you win their respect and trust? Or would they make their excuses and hurry away?

Unless you have something truly interesting and valuable to say when you join a conversation, you'll find people can hardly wait to get away from you. You and your carefully prepared messages will be left standing alone with no one to listen.

So what should you, as a B2B solution provider, do instead?

Start by listening

If you listen carefully to the conversations going on in the market you can learn a great deal about what people think of your company, as well as its products and services. A company that is open-minded and ready to learn will be able to more quickly correct mismatches between its behavior and the preferences of the market, and adapt to coming changes in buyer priorities and behavior, innovating across almost every aspect of its business.

What should you listen for? Here's a list of thought-starters:

Expressed needs	Financial considerations
Desires and wants	Technical considerations
Corporate culture issues	Names of key clients and prospects
Concerns	Channel partners
Complaints	Regulatory agencies
Problems	Legislators
Compliments	Timing requirements
Competitive activity	Corporate mandates
Your own product and organization names	Preferred supplier specifications
Key competitor product and organization names	Procurement processes
Industry and category keywords	Resource considerations
Hurdles and roadblocks	In-house skillsets
Attributes of special value	Existing contracts
Customer service concerns	Influential journalists and bloggers
Maintenance requirements	New book releases
Strategic considerations	Other topics relevant to your industry
Politics and policies	

Figure 2.5 Things to listen for in Voice of Customer contexts.

Most listening is part of a lengthy process. Occasionally, however, the payoff can be immediate. Casey Hibbard, author of the e-book "Stories that Sell", provides us with an example of how one tweet set up a six-figure deal for a B2B company, US-based communication solutions provider Avaya, Inc.

Avaya uses Radian6 technology to provide a dashboard of mentions that include not just Avaya's own name, but the names of competitors, competing products and other important key words or phrases. When members of Avaya's social media team "hear" something that may be relevant, the appropriate person or department within the company is alerted. A decision is then made whether a response would be a good idea. None of Avaya's "couple of dozen" weekly responses are automatically generated—instead, they are all crafted as genuine dialogue with a person or company. Listening also brings sales opportunities, such as when a tweet was noticed that posed the question: "shoretel or avaya? Time for a new phone system very soon".

Within 15 minutes, Avaya's staff had responded, inviting the tweeter to call the company and be put in touch with someone who could help him with his decision. Thirteen days later, Avaya's business partner closed a USD 250,000 sale. And the customer later tweeted: "… we have selected AVAYA as our new phone system. Excited by the technology and benefits …"

Listening for just 10 minutes a day

A common concern about monitoring Voice of Customer goings-on is that it takes up too much time.

According to the team at HubSpot, however, it's entirely possible for one person to keep an eye on things. If you set up a solid routine, monitoring your online presence doesn't have to be a hassle at all. Here's HubSpot's advice:

1. **Check Twitter for chatter about your company (2 minutes):**
   Use tools like tweetbeep.com or search.twitter.com to monitor conversations about your company in real-time. To check once a day, set up an RSS feed for a specific Twitter Search to go straight to your Google Reader. Do this by clicking the little RSS icon after you complete a search. Now, ongoing search results will be sent to your reader.

2. **Scan Google Alerts (1.5 minutes):** Check your Google Alerts (alerts.google.com) for your chosen terms selected from the thought-starters shown above. To set this up, enter your search terms and select to receive updates as they happen or once daily. Now, when people blog about your products or related keywords, an alert will be sent to your inbox. You can read the articles and respond right away!

3. **Check Facebook stats (1 minute):** Visit your Company Page's Facebook Insights. This can be found by clicking "more" under the page's main photo. Scan your fans and page views count. If you are a member of a group, check to see if any new discussions started.

4. **Answer industry-related LinkedIn questions (3 minutes):** Search for questions on LinkedIn that you or members of your company can answer. You can set up an RSS feed for specific question categories to go to your Google Reader as well. When you find a relevant question, respond and include a link to your website.

5. **Use Google Reader (reader.google.com) to check Flickr, Delicious, Digg and others (2.5 minutes):** Also set up RSS feeds for searches on your company name and industry terms on other social media sites. Similar to monitoring LinkedIn and Twitter, your Reader will serve as a great place to centralize your other searches too!

If doing the above in just 10 minutes seems like a wild exaggeration, it probably is (especially if you factor in the time it takes to determine and formulate appropriate responses to whatever you may find). You cannot, of course, listen to everyone—not in ten minutes a day, not even in ten hours a day. Some corporate prioritization is required.

Listening to key influencers

If your industry is awash with buyer conversations, and your marketing department small, then prioritizing who you listen to is a must. Where there may be 20,000 people involved in more or less relevant conversations, a much smaller number of key influencers—perhaps no more than 100—will likely have a disproportionate influence on prospects and clients. Keeping tabs on that small group of influencers would be a very effective substitute for monitoring everyone.

You probably already know some of them personally—and others by reputation. They're the people who always seem to know what's going on in your industry, and typically have an opinion. Perhaps they write a column for your trade magazine, or are usually interviewed by journalists seeking an industry viewpoint. Or perhaps it's the journalists themselves who should be considered influencers because they specialize in (and have an intelligent understanding of) your industry sector.

Your goal should be to identify the most-followed commentators and build relationships with that group. The influencers of whom you're probably least aware, however, are what we'll call Digital Influencers. They man the digital outposts (on Facebook, Twitter and the blogs), sharing their opinions on the latest and greatest happenings in their spheres of interest. As you begin identifying possible candidates for your influencer lists, consider these further perspectives from Sparxoo:

Identifying influencers
Influencers come in all different shapes and sizes. There are cultural influencers, political influencers, and even those kids who often exert decision-making powers in their household. Each individual or group of influencer(s) requires a smart, tailored communications approach.

Identifying how you're going to reach influencers is essential in building long-lasting relationships. Are you going to be speaking with, through or to them? Knowing this will help shape your bond with influencers and form your strategy.

To begin thinking about influencers, consider:

- Their passion point(s)—do they focus all of their time on your entrepreneurial passion, or do they have several areas of expertise?

- The degrees of separation from the decision maker(s)—different people and organizations exert different types of influence.

- How can they benefit from your initiative? Think of ways to motivate your target influencers to get behind your product.

Compiling your influencer list

Start by writing down a few names of influencers within your industry. Look back through trade magazines, recent reviews or industry conferences. Identify those serving in voluntary positions on industry associations or as judges at relevant awards. Talk to your clients and ask whose views they most respect.

Once you've created a first draft, you'll want to prioritize the names. Consider these factors as you review the main contenders:

- **How many relevant people do they influence?**
  Typically, that's a function of the platform through which their views are published—a trade magazine columnist might be more influential with your target market than a newspaper columnist with a larger but far more diverse readership.

- **To what degree do they influence their audience?**
  When their view on a particular topic is published, does that become the accepted wisdom or is it merely a minority opinion?

- **How influential is their audience?**
  Are they read by CEOs or by operational personnel—and which segment is more important to you?

When it comes to automating the process of listening to online conversations, you will need to consult experts in the field. That's because you're likely to need a good deal of guidance in choosing between the many free or inexpensive tools that can identify influencers and rank their relative influence, and more expensive but highly effective tools such as Salesforce's Radian6. Such tools are typically US-centric, but might be worth reviewing, depending on where your geographic influence is strongest.

Once you do find your influencers, some words of advice from *Maria Ogneva* on The Social Customer:

- Research each influencer thoroughly.
- Never pitch, but rather build a relationship over time.
- Ensure that the relationship makes sense, and that your product is aligned with this person's interests.
- Invite them "behind the scenes" and collaborate with them on the ideal product. They are often experts, and want their opinions to be respected and considered. Besides, you will get some great feedback early.
- Send them products ahead of the general release time (where relevant).

In general, you should adopt the philosophy of cultivating meaningful relationships with influencers, and leaving them to communicate in turn to their followers (your prospective customers). A note of caution: avoid offering any form of inducement to these influencers. Apart from potentially offending them and generating adverse comment, you'll find that in the interests of transparency most will be required to declare such offerings—rendering any subsequent recommendations suspect.

So when is it safe to talk to prospects directly?

We've already seen that salespeople are largely undesirable intruders in this phase of the information-gathering process. That said, however, it is possible to participate in the Voice of Customer process provided that you are speaking objectively, in Voice of Industry mode, rather than as a commercially tainted representative of the company.

Which leads us on to the topic of our next chapter.

Key take-outs

- Customers are talking among themselves.

- Buyers don't just follow conversations, they start them.

- A number of buyer roles impact on the decision-making process.

- People tend to trust the wisdom of crowds.

- The type of information sought by prospective purchasers depends on where they are in the purchasing process.

- Less than a third of buyers think salespeople are helpful.

- The conversations taking place online and in the marketplace will tell you nearly everything you need to know about your company and your customers.

- Your key role in the Voice of Customer arena is to listen and respond.

- Identify the key influencers in Voice of Customer forums and build meaningful relationships with them.

Questions for B2B strategists

- What are the buying processes of your various customer types? How have these changed over time?

- Has your sales team's approach changed to reflect the changes in today's buying processes?

- Think about your team's sales approach. Are prospective buyers likely to think they are helpful or just hard-selling?

- Who are the key influencers in your industry? What sort of relationship might you be able to build with them? What could be in it for them?

Notes

Voice of Industry

Independent content & engagement

VOICE OF INDUSTRY: Where companies and experts communicate about solutions and industry-level matters without directly pushing branded products and services.

46

CHAPTER THREE

Voice of Industry

What does it take to speak with a Voice of Industry?

The overall purpose of the Voice of Industry efforts you are about to set in motion is to strengthen the company's reputation as a trusted source of information and advice about your industry and the solutions it can provide. Handled correctly, this strategy will lead to your company building relationships with many prospects and helping to shape their views well before they're visible on your competitors' radars.

Speaking with a Voice of Industry, and having people listen to and respect your opinions, doesn't require some sort of election or coronation that specially selects your company for the role. Simply start producing valuable, objective advice—distilling your years of experience into insights that are of relevance to your prospective customers—and offer those materials freely to everyone.

...

"The moment you stop mentioning your products and services by name is the moment you shift from being a salesperson to being an advocate."

Social Media Examiner's Michael Stelzner

...

Your content should comprise the sorts of topics we canvassed in Chapter Two—those which are relevant to prospects doing their preliminary and follow-up research—as well as any key issues unearthed during your on-going monitoring of Voice of Customer activities.

One common difficulty we've noticed as companies make the transition to Voice of Industry communications: they struggle to achieve the most suitable tone and style for today's B2B buyer. If your marketing and communications departments have become accustomed to churning out company-oriented, product-based texts, videos and events, it can be tough to break the habit. What's required is a more neutral, journalistic style, varying depending on the type of message being communicated. We all come across this style almost every day—when we read Voice of Industry publications in our own industries or when catching up with national and international news commentary. Breaking long-established practices within the corporation, however, may require a complete change of content supplier and editor. You may also find it necessary to educate upper management on the new Voice, changing editing and review practices from the top down.

In what formats should you create your chosen content? We'll cover that in more detail in a later chapter, but for now consider the possibilities listed below:

Distributed as blog posts, magazine columns, syndicated articles, white papers, e-books and newsletters:

- How-to articles

- Answers to common queries and problems

- Case studies and other success stories

- Interviews with key industry figures (both internal and external)

- Trends and statistics

- Need analyses

- Solution comparisons

- Reports of surveys

Distributed via multimedia:

- YouTube videos

- Podcasts

- PowerPoint presentations

Distributed via social media:

- Tweets about hot topics
- Answers to questions on LinkedIn
- Latest industry news on Facebook

Distributed via webinars and live events:

- Workshops and seminars

The vital ingredient across all of these formats: an objective, uncommercialized (or at least not hard-selling) perspective on the issues that matter to your industry's customers.

Media choices for Voice of Industry

Today's B2B marketers have a broader range of media options than ever. To help make sense of all these options, it's useful to make a distinction between *paid*, *owned* and *earned* media. If you're unfamiliar with the terminology, a few words of explanation are in order.

Paid media needs little introduction: it's the stuff we all think of as traditional opportunities to advertise. And it's typically where propaganda-style messages rear their ugly heads. In traditional media, this includes the usual suspects such as magazine and newspaper advertisements and TV and radio spots; in new media, think banner advertising, Google Adwords, Facebook ads, pre-roll video ads and all the other executions for which you pay a fee.

Propaganda, and the media forms commonly used to promote it, as you've probably gathered by now, are not the focus of this book. That said, paid media does have an important role to play—particularly when you are starting out with a Three Voices™ strategy. It's a key tool for building initial attention for and attracting subscribers to your Voice of Industry activities, whether you are launching a thought leadership site or a newsletter discussing industry topics. In the medium to long term, however, you should aim to heavily reduce or even phase out paid media from your media mix (at least for Voice of Industry initiatives).

Of greater importance, seen from a Three Voices™ perspective is *earned* media. We use this term to describe coverage you gain in spaces you don't fully control—for example, when happy/unhappy customers blog or tweet about your products or services, when journalists report about you (whether through traditional or digital media) or when influential commentators talk about your products or services to their fans and followers. To our way of thinking, earned media also encompasses the communities, channels and so on you may have set up using Facebook, LinkedIn or YouTube, for example. The unifying principle with earned media is that you have earned your place in the media landscape based on something you've done or content you have created.

Owned media is different—it's material and interactions you create yourself, in a company-controlled context. So corporate blogs, offline seminars, microsites, interactive publications and the like are examples of owned media—you are able to fully determine the content and interactions because you own the medium. This level of control makes owned media the alpha and omega for your Voice of Industry efforts.

Now let's take a closer look at earned and owned media—the focal points of your Voice of Industry.

Earned media

There are three categories of earned media that are of particular interest for your Voice of Industry activities:

Independent, content-hungry publications

In most industries, numerous online and offline trade publications carry news and information about the sector. The offshore wind energy industry, for example, has many such publications, including Offshorewind.biz and UKOffshoreWind.com. Similarly, much of the food industry keeps up with the play via FoodNavigator.com and that site's many associated publications addressing industry sub-categories such as baked goods. There are also trade associations or government agencies that publish deep and wide on industry matters—such as the European Wind Energy Association (www.ewea.org). These are cross-industry media commonly assumed to be independent of any single vendor's influence.

Relationships with, and paid or earned presence in such publications are a key strategic component when you want your organization to take on the mantle of Voice of Industry, and to become one of the key influencers in your product or service category. You will need to cultivate these relationships, forming close bonds with journalists and editors in the same way as you would when implementing any traditional PR strategy—but with the emphasis on providing "neutral" yet compelling content that adds value at an industry or solution level. Make an effort to understand what type of content interests them most, and be sure to create a two-way flow of visitors wherever you can. Occasionally, great content pieces might even capture the attention of an influential blogger, but you shouldn't expect a similar on-going relationship can be built with him or her.

Operated but not owned platforms

Many B2B companies have chosen to center their online marketing activities around platforms that, in reality, are owned and controlled by other entities. In this context, therefore, earned media refers to presence your efforts have created on platforms such as LinkedIn, Facebook or YouTube—all of which are at the mercy of the platform owner rather than under your own control. While such platforms are useful for your Three Voices™ strategy, their primary role, in most cases, should be to direct traffic to media whose formats, functions and audiences you do, in fact, have control over.

Content sharing partnerships

If you're looking to get more bang for your buck, then content sharing with non-competing companies, suppliers, implementation partners, regulatory bodies and similar that share the same target audiences can be very useful. For example:

- The commercial section of a bank writes a monthly column for an accounting firm's newsletter.

- A manufacturer provides industry-level articles for use by its channel partners, and they provide customer case stories to the manufacturer.

- An expert in food packaging is on a food industry blogger panel run by a manufacturer of food ingredients.

Taking such partnerships to the nth degree, some companies create highly effective "content rings", where visitors to a blog, for example, once they have finished reading a particular article are encouraged to read a new article featured on the blog of another company in the ring. Finishing that article, the next item of interest appears on yet another company's blog within the ring. After viewing perhaps five articles, each sending you to a different site, you will most likely find yourself back on the blog where you began your journey. Tactics like these can enable companies in a ring to dominate search results—and your impression of which players are the leaders in the industry.

Is the practice ethical? Is it cheating? A word of warning: Google regularly penalizes sites and brands who engage in black-bag SEO tactics such as cash-for-links schemes, bumping them down in the page ranking system and excluding them from search results for a period of time. For this reason, and to follow good commercial practice in everything your company does, the emphasis must be placed on quality content partnerships instead of artificial link networks (such as paid "link farms") designed to overly manipulate natural search rankings. We know of quite large enterprises that have had their rankings severly reduced overnight as a result of changes to Google's search algorithms, requiring them to rebuild much of their online presence from the ground up.

Owned media

So much for earned media. What we believe you should focus your future activities upon, however, are any industry-level media your company is able to build and own itself, mimicking the tone and style of independent publications but providing a much more controllable and data-rich platform for engaging with stakeholders of all kinds.

Imagine the following scenario. An HR manager for a company you would really like to have on your client list is cruising her favorite industry news and resource sites. She is, of course, also performing keyword searches via Google. She's looking for a solution exactly like the one you provide. And no, she didn't go to your company's website as a starting point for her search. Instead, her initial aim is to gather broad knowledge about the latest solutions, their advantages and disadvantages—well before visiting any vendor websites or calling the salespeople of a few select vendors whose solutions look the most promising. In particular, she is exploring industry news and resource sites to get hints, tips and recommendations from experts or users—not to hear propaganda-laden messages from someone or something focused on making a sale (i.e. your company in its old communications model).

This is where your Voice of Industry strategy comes into play: providing the HR manager with your company's views on her challenges, and the reasoning behind the solutions and approaches the company believes buyers like her should adopt. Many companies who have already realized the value of communicating with this Voice are busy working with paid and, whenever possible, earned media to get noticed out there. They may also operate a mild form of owned (usually offline) media by hosting seminars around topics of interest (a tactic heavily deployed by law and accounting firms, in particular).

For more advanced B2B organizations, however, a more effective utilization of the Voice of Industry strategy will move beyond trying to place your company's content on existing industry news and resource sites. The preferred alternative: owning and operating at least one optimized Voice of Industry publication platform yourself.

A point of clarification: when we use the word "publication", we're not just talking about a newsletter or magazine—the sort of thing people normally think of when the term is used. Instead, we think of today's B2B brands as publishers, creating a steady stream of tailored content that addresses the needs of prospects and seeks to influence their likes and dislikes.

By this new definition, a website is a publication. So is a newsletter or magazine, whether offline or online. And the list doesn't stop there. Taking things a step further, we're not that interested in talking about individual pieces of content, but encourage companies to think in terms of "conversations". For example, the launch of a new product is one big conversation about the problem or opportunity the product addresses, how these issues are addressed and so on. It's a conversation that is spread through various types of content (white papers, videos, brochures) in Voice of Industry and Voice of Company contexts. And this conversation can occur across a multitude of devices and events—preferably accessible in any format, context or on any device that your stakeholders use to access information.

So what might an online, company-owned and operated Voice of Industry activity look like? To start with, it could be centered around a website with its own, industry-related name. For example, a manufacturer of commercial life rafts could call its Voice of Industry site something along the lines of *"Which Liferaft?"*.

Another example is that of Denmark's highly successful Saxo Bank, which owns and operates a site called *Tradingfloor.com*, bearing the signature (in fine print) "powered by Saxo Bank". Monthly visits to the site, and leads generated, are said to number in the tens of thousands. While, in this case, the website is what we would describe as the "core destination" for the bank's Voice of Industry, some of the most enthusiastic users of Tradingfloor.com's insights may never visit the site itself, instead interacting via Twitter, LinkedIn or other media facilitated by the bank.

There are many ways to approach a Voice of Industry effort. For example, shipping giant A.P. Moller-Maersk launched a campaign website around the message that it's "time for the industry to change its ways" (www.changingthewaywethinkaboutshipping.com). The site contains such items as carefully crafted company statements, published press articles, a video of the company's CEO speaking on the subject at an industry conference and so on. Importantly, the company uses its Voice of Industry site to invite others in the industry to join the effort to change the industry—customers, employees and competitors alike. Rather than being a dynamic content resource, the site is a one-off, static site designed as an element within a larger campaign toolbox.

CASE STUDY

KINAXIS'S SUPPLY CHAIN EXPERT COMMUNITY

One company that has deeply embraced a Voice of Industry approach (even if the company doesn't use this particular terminology) is Kinaxis. This Canadian provider of supply chain management solutions operates a three-legged online strategy based on content, community and comedy that has delivered excellent results for the company:

- 2.7 times more traffic to Kinaxis.com

- 3.2 times more conversions (leads)

- 5.3 times increase in traffic to the Kinaxis blog/community

Ray Schultz of TellAllMarketing describes the three components of the Kinaxis strategy:

The Blog

Front and center was the 21st Century Supply Chain Blog (https://community.kinaxis.com/index.jspa). The company recruited 21 authors from executives to supply chain experts. They contribute case histories, links to interesting sites and trade show reports. "We shoot for a blog posting a day," noted Kirsten Watson, director of corporate marketing for Kinaxis. "We don't always hit it." The blog is syndicated on the firm's community, and on third-party sites. It ranks at the top with many important keywords.

LinkedIn

Through studies into the supply chain marketplace conducted by *Forrester Research*, Kinaxis found that its audience is "heavily engaged online"—70 percent seek work-related information and news over the Web, and 20 percent use sites like LinkedIn and Wikipedia at least once a week. As Watson put it, Kinaxis "took Forrester's recommendation to go where the fish are." That meant finding supply chain groups on LinkedIn. "We watched content, seeing how active people were, how many were actually engaged," she said. "Out of many groups, we settled on 46." From there, the company syndicated its blog, and posted links to its content library. It posts often on core topics, drawing dozens of comments per day.

"It's important to stay on top of them," Watson said. In addition to finding ideas for content, the company gets a "sense of what's going on in the marketplace."

Online Community

The third part of the Kinaxis online tripod is the firm's Supply Chain Expert Community. Launched in 2009, "it has brought us to point where we have critical mass," Watson said. Watson described the community as a "content-rich home for supply chain experts to learn, share and connect." Members can add content, seek advice, browse for colleagues and read expert bloggers. "At the end of the day, the community is owned by the members, not by Kinaxis," Watson adds.

Members can get also a laugh from Suitemates, the firm's online comedy show. In a typical episode, two convicted executives blame their plight on a salesman who never says no. "This suite will make me a sandwich?" someone asks him in a flashback. "Yes!" "This suite gives land back to the Indians?" "Yes!"

Current membership count for the Supply Chain Expert Community: over 6000. This is one strategy that clearly works.

Let's consider more closely the hypothetical life raft example mentioned earlier. *Which Liferaft?* could be a shipping industry-specific site containing articles, videos, guest columns and similar designed to help ship-owners navigate the world of marine safety equipment. Content could come from a wide variety of sources both internal and external to the manufacturer itself. Topics could include trends, technical developments, products, maintenance and service. In contrast to the relaxed dialogue one might expect in a Voice of Customer context, content is polished and well presented. Articles have been professionally edited. Opinions presented are those of industry experts, some of whom may be, for example, R&D employees from within the company. There are written and videoed interviews, often in the form of podcasts.

Which Liferaft? would be entirely managed by the manufacturer itself—which means, quite simply, that despite there being a great deal of input from sources external to the company, the manufacturer gets to choose which content gets pride of place. The company appears discreetly on the site's front page as the sponsor of the site, but gives up center stage to discussions of industry topics rather than company-centric sales and marketing messages.

The aim is, of course, to build a large and growing audience of customers, prospects and influencers who visit this site on a regular basis. That's why the company should also plan to fuel the site with membership drives in many of its other marketing and communication activities—and why its Voice of Industry site would need various forms of regular external communication (such as a newsletter, blogs, tweets) that strengthen the relationship between the site and its visitors. Cross-pollination of content with external Voice of Industry sites and offline forums would also play a part. In the long run, activities might include webinars, offline seminars, perhaps even an annual *Which Liferaft?* conference.

In the fictional Which Liferaft example, we've decided the manufacturer should own the underlying Voice of Industry platform, giving its marketing department greater control over content and better access to traffic data. But the degree to which your company's brand and products appear on an owned media site and whether this level of visible presence is appropriate will depend on the type of product or service you offer. Of course, transparency is important— never try to hide your company's identity completely (a practice that is illegal in many parts of the world). Saxo Bank has chosen to appear with an almost equal amount of branding present on both its Voice of Industry content site (www.tradingfloor.com) and its company website (www.saxobank.com). The essential difference is in the way that Saxo Bank makes its messages a little more useful, usable and enjoyable on tradingfloor.com than on its corporate website. In the bank's case, working in a regulated industry means that the bank's own Voice of Company presence appears more strongly on its Voice of Industry site than would be required of companies working in a non-regulated industry.

A Voice of Industry site of the type we've discussed here is a highly useful tool for persuading the new breed of B2B buyer. In fact, ITSMA/PAC research conducted in 2010 discovered that some 65 percent of B2B buyers were willing to engage with vendor-sponsored communities, following discussions and posting questions.

CASE STUDY

LET'S HEAR IT FOR OTICON

In the world of hearing aids, Oticon is one of the largest and most influential manufacturers. Its target market comprises consumers who use its hearing instruments (B2C) and the hearing healthcare professionals who serve them (B2B). Earning the respect and attention of both groups is crucial for Oticon's continued success.

The Ida Institute (www.idainstitute.com) is an independent, not-for-profit educational institute located north of Copenhagen, Denmark. Enabled by the Oticon Foundation, the institute's mission and content are aimed at providing insight and "a more holistic understanding of the complex journey of hearing loss to better assist hearing care professionals and hearing-impaired persons". The institute generates and disseminates practical and actionable knowledge, organized around collaborative learning. Activities are designed to facilitate exchange among thought leaders, scholars, practitioners, educators and professional advocacy groups.

Here's an excerpt from the institute's website:

"We collaborate with hearing care professionals and academics from around the world to identify needs in the field of audiology and develop tools and strategies to meet those needs. Our seminars invite members from the hearing care community to come together to advance thinking about hearing loss and to develop insights, strategies, and practical tools that can be implemented in clinical and educational settings. Through our seminars, workshops, E-Learning Lab and interactive website, we facilitate knowledge exchanges and host 'conversations that matter' within the hearing care community."

The institute's director, Lise Lotte Bundesen, heads a staff that reflects the institute's commitment to exploring a wide range of approaches—communication specialist, audiologist, learning specialist, concept designer and even anthropologists.

Oticon's presence on the Ida Institute site is carefully limited, making the institute a clear, arms-length Voice of Industry activity and ensuring the highest level of credibility. Adding to this credibility is the institute's largely independent advisory board, which comprises eight distinguished experts in hearing health and related disciplines. The board provides counsel and support for the institute's strategic planning, including seminar topics, content and structure, faculty appointments and dissemination of its information and tools.

While its presence is appropriately discreet, the Oticon brand makes its appearance via the Oticon Foundation, which is publicly thanked on the institute's site for its "generous support". How useful to Oticon's sales of hearing instruments is this Voice of Industry? While there may not be any publicly accessible data on the institute's membership numbers (reported as over 5000 on the site itself), revenues generated, impact on Oticon's brand equity, or the number of leads it may generate, it's hard to imagine that the participation of and input from what has become a large, captive community of B2B buyers would be other than welcomed by the wider Oticon organization.

There's another upside for B2B companies working with a Voice of Industry approach—and that's the effect on the culture of the company itself. Owning and operating a Voice of Industry website seems to open the minds of both management and employees to new possibilities (even if customers don't go so far as to disrupt or reinvent the whole business model). Voice of Industry sites typically create new partnerships between the company and external industry experts and thought leaders. And adopting a Voice of Industry perspective involves the company in a mission that helps to promote the industry as a whole—which is good for everybody.

Of course, at some point the imperative kicks in to actually sell some products— which brings us to our next focus: Voice of Company.

Key take-outs

- Voice of Industry carries greater credibility than Voice of Company.

- To speak with a Voice of Industry you need to produce valuable, objective advice and opinions, and offer that insight without charge.

- There are many different formats for Voice of Industry content.

- B2B businesses need to use a combination of paid, owned and earned media:

  o Paid media includes trade ads, banner advertising and Adwords.

  o Owned media refers to what we create ourselves in spaces we control.

  o Earned media is coverage we gain in spaces we don't control.

- Paid media is useful for growing the number of visits and registrations in connection with your owned Voice of Industry activities.

- With owned media, a key aim is to build a large and growing audience within a controlled content environment.

- Research indicates some 65% of B2B buyers are willing to engage with vendor-sponsored communities, following discussions and posting questions.

- Incorporating Voice of Industry can have a positive effect on your company's culture, creativity and processes.

Questions for B2B strategists

- Is your company running websites, workshops, webinars or other events based around industry-level topics?

- Does your company cultivate a database of members or subscribers for this type of event?

- What might happen if you moved your events closer to Voice of Industry principles? Could you form better connections with more potential buyers or key influencers?

- Is your sales and marketing organization ready to adopt the role of customer advocate instead of salesperson?

Notes

Voice of
Company

Company-centric
communication

Voice of Company: Messages and media clearly designed to promote the company and its branded products and services.

CHAPTER FOUR

Voice of Company

The importance of your digital identity

You may be aware of the classic *McGraw-Hill* advertisement promoting that company's business magazines. Now more than fifty years old, the ad still resonates with B2B marketers around the world. It depicts a business prospect announcing to a visiting salesperson:

> "*I don't know who you are.*
> *I don't know your company.*
> *I don't know your company's product.*
> *I don't know what your company stands for.*
> *I don't know your company's customers.*
> *I don't know your company's record.*
> *I don't know your company's reputation.*
> *Now—what was it you wanted to sell me?"*

MORAL: Sales start **before** your salesman calls—with business publication advertising.

McGRAW-HILL MAGAZINES
BUSINESS · PROFESSIONAL · TECHNICAL

Source: © The McGraw-Hill Companies, Inc.
Reproduced with the permission of The McGraw-Hill Companies, Inc.

Figure 4.1 The classic *McGraw-Hill* advertisement.

Some things have changed in the last half-century. Nowadays, a prospective customer will know rather more about you (although what they know is usually out of your control). Before deciding whether or not even to include you on his or her shortlist, your prospect will know (or can quickly find out):

- The style and substance of your organization
- What Google thinks about you and your organization
- Whether or not you are contributing to your industry or the community
- How your reputation stacks up on LinkedIn and how well-connected you are
- What your peers, customers and competitors are blogging or tweeting about you
- How current or former clients rate your products or services

If there are any stains on your digital record, they'll quickly be uncovered. If you're invisible online, that will be evident as well.

We've already discussed the importance of supporting your digital identity through appropriate participation in Voice of Customer and Voice of Industry initiatives. There comes a time, however, when the prospect wants to know even more about you. If you've done your groundwork correctly, that prospect will already have a favorable opinion. Now it's time to support and close the sale with your Voice of Company.

Give them what they want

Of course, no one is born with an instinctive, unquestioning need for your product or service. So they are unlikely to come knocking on your company's door to purchase whatever you have to sell at whatever price you ask.

In a competitive situation, with perhaps four or five B2B suppliers offering solutions to a prospective customer, there are likely to be several major questions in the latter's mind. For example, "which basic type of solution is best suited for my needs? What can go wrong with this type of solution and how might I avoid the pitfalls? What might it be like to be a customer of Company XYZ? Do they honor their warranties?"

B2B buyers constantly seek reassurance before they make their purchases. And these days they judge your company more than ever on two key points: what your content says about you, and what other people say about you.

Ideally, your Voice of Company content should be perceived as knowledgeable, helpful, honest and open-minded. It should offer insights and inspiration in addition to the usual information about your specific offerings. Its tone and style should be relaxed yet respectful, rather than formal and distant. Your content should clearly show that you think in terms of your customers and their realities rather than your own. And it should appear in media regularly consumed and respected by your audiences.

Which media? A study of European B2B Buyers (*BuyerSphere Report 2011: The annual survey of changing B2B buyer behavior*) provides useful guidance, identifying which sources prospective buyers consult when making their final supplier choice.

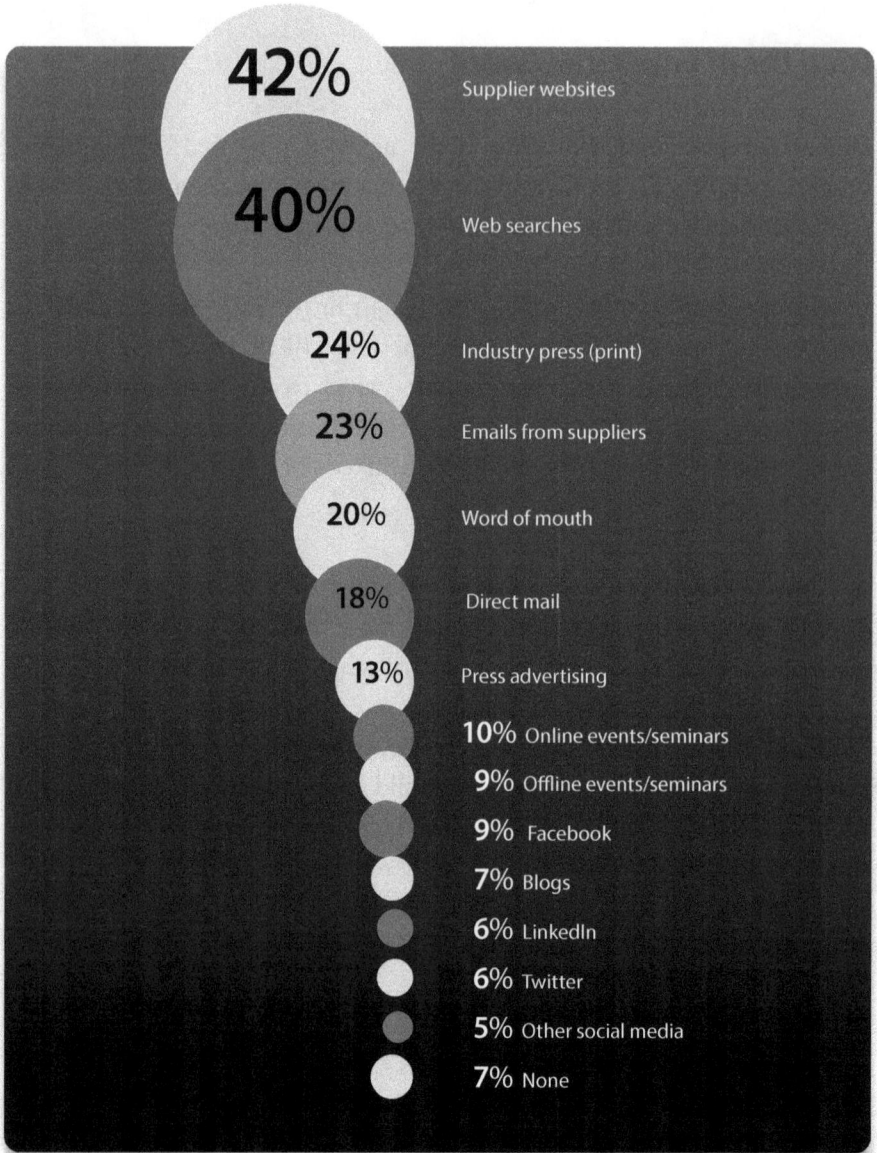

42%	Supplier websites
40%	Web searches
24%	Industry press (print)
23%	Emails from suppliers
20%	Word of mouth
18%	Direct mail
13%	Press advertising
10%	Online events/seminars
9%	Offline events/seminars
9%	Facebook
7%	Blogs
6%	LinkedIn
6%	Twitter
5%	Other social media
7%	None

Source: BuyerSphere Report 2011: The annual survey of changing B2B buyer behavior

Figure 4.2 Information sources used in selecting final suppliers.

To some, the preceding chart may seem to contradict earlier statements about the role of the company's own communications in buyer decision-making processes. But it's important to realize that here we're talking about the habits of buyers who have already been out researching information from a variety of sources and who have now moved to a stage where it's time to connect directly with the vendors themselves.

As these results indicate, it's vital for vendors to have an effective website—and to be easily found for prospect-focused keywords and phrases on search engines. Beyond those touchpoints, however, it's also important for the company to be well represented in both paid and earned media. Your Voice of Industry initiatives should stand your brand in good stead in search and in earned media—but you will have to indulge in some more traditional promotion of your specific products along the way, to ensure that they are represented appropriately when prospects come calling.

What sort of information should you be providing through your Voice of Company websites? The correct answer to that question will depend in large part on the outcome of your Voice of Customer listening activities. As you ponder those results, however, consider these possibilities:

Company presentations	Company profile
Product background sheet	Product data sheets
Product specifications	Product safety data sheets
Product brochures	Product reviews
Product presentations	Technical reports/studies
White papers	Competitive comparisons
Case studies	Customer testimonials
Product videos	Frequently asked questions
Total Cost of Ownership data	Return on Investment analyses

Figure 4.3 Information choices for Voice of Company contexts.

When considering your content, you might also like to take note of the attributes that B2B buyers have historically taken into account when evaluating suppliers. Technology may have intruded since this data was first published (in April 1974), but human nature persists.

ATTRIBUTES USED TO EVALUATE SUPPLIERS

1. Overall reputation of the supplier

2. Financing terms

3. Supplier's flexibility in adjusting to purchasing organization's needs

4. Experience with the supplier in similar situations

5. Technical service offered

6. Confidence in the salespeople

7. Convenience of placing the order

8. Data on reliability of the product

9. Price

10. Technical specifications

11. Ease of operation or use

12. Preferences of principal user of the product

13. Training offered by the supplier

14. Training time required

15. Reliability of delivery date promised

16. Ease of maintenance

17. Sales service expected after date of purchase

Source: Donald R Lehmann and John O'Shaughnessy, "Difference in Attribute Importance for Different Industrial Products", Journal of Marketing 1974, American Marketing Association

Figure 4.4 Attributes typically used to evaluate suppliers.

Preparing your Voice of Company

Despite the changes we've been discussing in the ways that B2B buyers gather information and make purchasing decisions, most companies still rely solely on their Voice of Company and their sales force to reach and persuade prospective customers. For various reasons, often budget and/or know-how related, they are stuck in the old paradigm, with communication activities that center around propaganda-style websites, brochures, press releases, trade show stands and similar traditional solutions.

If your company falls into this unfortunate category, all is not lost. There's work to do to get your house in order before embarking on a Three Voices™ strategy, but many of the activities you've been doing can continue in their present form; others may simply require fine-tuning or extension to meet the demands of the new paradigm.

So how do we recommend you prepare your Voice of Company to play a more effective role?

Drop the propaganda

Naturally, the first and most important change when preparing your Voice of Company as a solid pillar of a Three Voices™ strategy is to remove as much as possible of what your prospects and customers might view as propaganda. Search your texts for words like "cutting edge", "world-class", "market-leading", "groundbreaking", and their slogan-spouting friends. Review every claim, asking yourself whether it adds value to those who read your marketing materials— or whether you are simply creating an unbelievable image of perfection that clashes with the opinions customers or prospects may already have formed in Voice of Customer contexts.

It's not easy to decide how far to go with reducing propaganda-like messages. In our experience, the best way is to talk with your marketing and communication suppliers about establishing a set of guidelines, then allow them to rework your materials until the right tone and delivery of value is achieved.

Create an effective value proposition

Have you clearly stated your company's promise to the market? There can be many attributes for which you may wish to be known: established, big, international, knowledge-based, leading in technology, one-stop shop, good at customer service, reliable, fast, a good citizen, trusted, open, and the like. But if you attempt to claim these all at once, your messages will lose impact and memorability. That's where your value proposition plays its part, telling your market what value you can bring to them and how you are different from everyone else.

Of course there are many B2B companies out there doing very nicely, thank you, without a clear value proposition. In our view, their success has often been built upon good products and or services, and an effective sales force— two key growth drivers in the old world of business and still great assets in a world of heightened competition. We also believe that many of those companies would have achieved even more with a sharper promise of value to the market, strengthening their brands and positioning themselves for continued growth in a future where they are competing with not just one or two others making similar products, but with many rivals distributed around the globe.

When evaluating your company's value proposition to determine if it is powerful enough for an effective Voice of Company platform, there are many criteria to consider. Some of these include:

- Does your value proposition clearly identify what differentiates your offering from that of your competitors?
- Is it relevant to your most important customers?
- Does it add value to the organization and its customers?
- Will it encourage customers to pay a premium?
- Can it aid in the selling process?
- Does it build customer loyalty?
- Can it attract positive media interest?
- Does it attract meaningful strategic alliances?
- Can it attract and help to keep top talent?
- Does the proposition fit with your company values?
- Is it short and memorable?

Far too many value propositions promise the earth but fail to deliver—which means their claims are likely to reek of propaganda, of course. So perhaps the most important key to the success of your value proposition is the degree to which it is in line with the company's executed strategy and experienced culture (as opposed to the stated strategy and culture). In other words, does the value proposition reflect who your company really is and how it really works?

Develop a strong brand story and identity

All too often, B2B companies conduct lengthy management workshops to develop written value propositions, then proceed to broadcast these exact same statements to the market. But this kind of value proposition is an internal statement of corporate intent and direction. It still needs to be creatively interpreted into a compelling brand story which can serve as one of the cornerstones of your Three Voices™ strategy.

Much has been written in the literature about the creation of strong brand stories, and the verbal and visual expressions that help to tell such stories. We don't intend to provide an additional set of guidelines in this book, preferring instead to illustrate the role of the value proposition and its creative expression in the case story that follows.

Breathing new life into an unadventurous Voice of Company

When RESON A/S, a market leader in sonar equipment for underwater surveying, decided it was time to revitalize its business approach and organization, the company also seized the opportunity to redefine its Voice of Company.

Spurred on by intensifying competition, RESON sought to build upon a clear, consistent story that could inspire both the company's strategy and its marketing communications. While that's never as easy as it might sound, getting it right can provide significant benefits.

Prior to the revitalization effort, RESON was typical of most B2B companies—using product-oriented messages that addressed rational, technical buying criteria but which paid little attention to benefits. What was missing was a powerful brand story that could create consistent and compelling messages. Emotional bonding was out as well: RESON's Voice of Company was decidedly impersonal.

Branding-wise, RESON's competitors were all in the same boat. All three of the leading companies, RESON included, focused almost entirely on their products and featured an unexciting visual design. Here was a great opportunity for RESON to stand out from its competitors, looking like a market leader by creating the industry's most powerful Voice of Company.

Several specific opportunities for improvement were identified:

- There was no clear emotional element to the brand—a key driver of human decision-making.
- The company's brand DNA was undefined, meaning high costs and low impact when creating marketing campaigns and individual marketing elements.
- The tone and style of the company's presence, as expressed through its website and marketing materials, was somewhat dated and not that different from its competitors.
- While the company wanted to be seen as a leader, there were few supporting signals other than propaganda-like statements such as "RESON is the world leader...".
- Marketing messages and materials were company-centric rather than reflecting customer pains and priorities.

The new Voice of Company meant a shift from portraying RESON's customers as marine surveyors to describing them as "professional underwater explorers". Images of hardy, intelligent and impressive explorers such as Jacques Cousteau were used as reference points of this new, aspirational way of perceiving customers. The goal was to introduce a stronger emotional reason to engage with the company by showing that RESON understood the challenges and shared the dreams of its customers.

It followed then, that if RESON's customers were "explorers", then their work must involve going on "expeditions". Here was a universe in which you might imagine Sir Walter Scott and his men with all their equipment in packs and crates being hauled along by dog sleds, with Walt at the fore, battling his way through white-out snow to achieve the mission. As Walt unfortunately discovered, you have to be very well-prepared if you want your expedition to be a success. You have to be "Expedition-ready"—a phrase that subsequently became RESON's new slogan. It all fitted well with the company's new strategic objective of providing a complete package of equipment and services rather than equipment alone.

A new visual and verbal identity (a whole new "Voice of Company") was created to reflect the exciting world of the professional underwater explorer. Gone were the boring product shots that had peppered the company's marketing materials, and in their place were images of challenging expeditions and the explorers who met those challenges. Technical specifications and images were still easily accessible, of course, but visitors to RESON's corporate website or receiving printed materials first encountered an appealing and clearly differentiated brand.

Marketing impact made easier
What were the results of RESON's revamped Voice of Company? First, the clarity of the company's new value proposition has made creating a content strategy around its messages far easier. At the same time, the new "Expedition-ready" creative universe provides clear direction that makes it faster and easier to come up with inspiring ideas, choose compelling images, tell engaging stories and determine where best to share these tales.

The next steps for RESON's marketing communications are now underway. Voice of Industry activities are planned, based on customers contributing their own stories, videos and photographs of the product in action (something, in fact, they voluntarily began to do the moment the company's new corporate website was launched). Through it all, the new RESON Voice of Company brand story acts both as a consistent source of inspiration as well as virtual glue that keeps all the company's messages in a clear, logical context no matter where RESON and its products are encountered.

In search of content

One of the issues that quickly becomes apparent when implementing a Three Voices™ strategy is the overriding importance of content. Let's turn our attention now to content: what makes it valuable, the types of content B2B buyers most want and why it matters.

Key take-outs

- Before customers call you, even before you call them, they already know a great deal about you.

- What they know is beyond your control.

- If you make their shortlist, you need a Voice of Company that won't create a disconnect between what they already believe and the story you tell them.

- It's vital to maintain effective corporate websites—and be easily found via search.

- Create meaningful links between your Voice of Industry activities and the content on your Voice of Company websites.

- Use what you learn from your Voice of Customer activities to guide the content and functionality of your website and other materials.

- Preparing a strong Voice of Company begins with:

    o Reducing or eliminating propaganda.

    o Determining a powerful value proposition.

    o Addressing both rational and emotional motivators.

    o Developing a strong brand story and identity.

Questions for B2B strategists

- What impression of your company might you get if you were to take the same journey as prospective buyers? Start with a Google search and see where it takes you.

- Consider the results of the exercise above. Would your company make it onto your shortlist?

- Do you currently monitor buyer conversations and interactions to decide what content your corporate website should provide?

- Does your company currently conduct any Voice of Industry activities?

- Are you tracking buyer conversations or simply relying on direct dialogue for information about buyer needs and priorities?

- If you're considering a Three Voices™ strategy, is your value proposition clear, relevant and credible?

- Are your company's corporate and product brands well-defined? Do they form a cohesive image of your company that corresponds to market "truths"?

- Do your current advertising and media agency partners have the know-how to help you work with a Three Voices™ strategy?

Notes

CHAPTER FIVE

Creating content
for the three Voices

Before you start reading this chapter, we'd like to make something quite clear: Whenever we use the word "content" in a marketing context, we mean information and information-based experiences of all kinds—from written articles, data and infographics to interactive video, podcasts, learning tools and engaging competitions.

You may have heard the phrase "Content is King" being proclaimed from the podium at numerous seminars aimed at enlightening marketing and communication professionals about the virtues of going online with your communication strategy. Forget it—that mantra has all too quickly become old news, despite recently being elevated to a more impressive "Content is God" status.

Instead, make way for what may seem like even more hype but which is, in fact, a rather sharp observation expounded in 2011 by online marketing veteran Cory Doctorow:

"Conversation is King—content is just something to talk about."

Cory is one of the most renowned blogger/editors of the digital age. He promoted the Creative Commons license, shares the helm as co-editor of the culturally reflective blog Boing Boing and, in 2005, he achieved fame by exposing Sony Music's inclusion of potentially damaging software in its CDs. Cory's statement on conversation emphasizes the importance of getting people engaged with your company, using carefully crafted content as bait.

The No. 1 factor in B2B marketing success: engagement

Engagement has become a much-overused buzzword in cyberspace these days, inevitably attracting a backlash from the digitally jaded. But just ask your sales team who they would rather have asking them for a proposal: someone with whom they've never been in contact before, or a person with whom they've already had a number of useful conversations.

Engagement in the offline world translates into nicely warm prospects and the same is true online, which is why a Three Voices™ strategy, at its core, is all about enabling meaningful engagement between the company, its customers, prospects and other influencers.

HOW ENGAGEMENT CAN BE VERY PROFITABLE INDEED

A guest post on the HubSpot blog by Zack Urlocker (former VP of Products at MySQL) shows how effective (and profitable) engagement through content has become:

"When Sun Microsystems acquired MySQL in 2008, we applied the same techniques (inbound marketing through content and conversation) across Sun's entire product line of software, servers and storage. The results were significant. In the course of a year, we increased the lead volume by 100 times and created a pipeline of revenue approaching a $500 million annual run rate."

So, yes, it's worth the effort. And, because you'll want to know exactly what Zack and his team did, first for MySQL and then for Sun:

"We didn't have much of a marketing budget. However, we did have a large community of users that lent itself to inbound marketing techniques. We developed a comprehensive lead generation, nurturing and scoring machine that was fuelled by a rich content strategy that included blogs, white papers, and web seminars. Traffic to the content was driven by search engine optimization and Google AdWords. Over the course of several years, we grew MySQL revenues to $100 million, in part due to inbound marketing."

Effective engagement requires a well-constructed content strategy for the creation, delivery and control of useful, usable content. Every B2B company should use such a strategy as a core part of its overall communication strategy. *Kristina Halvorson* of Minnesota-based *Brain Traffic*, the author of *Content Strategy for the Web* (New Riders, 2009) suggests the following ten questions to help us think about content strategy:

What, why, how, for whom, by whom, with what,
when, where, how often, what next?

To that concise list you should add "how to measure". Then we're pretty much done. But Kristina also makes the excellent point that good content is useful, usable and *enjoyable*. Typically, for B2B clients, it's the last of these three adjectives that is particularly difficult to ensure. In part, that's because turning what might otherwise be dry information into an interesting, even fun, experience demands more time, better ideas and, yes, more money. But it's also the magic that really transforms the way that B2B buyers interact with your company.

Halvorson sums up the principle of an effective, engaging content strategy:

> "[A sound content strategy] plots an achievable roadmap for individuals and organizations to create and maintain content that audiences will actually care about. It provides specific, well-informed recommendations about how we're going to get from where we are today (no content, bad content, or too much content) to where we want to be (useful, usable content people will actually care about)."

In an ideal world, your company's content would be managed by a powerful content management system and a fully integrated and automated marketing system that could help you to analyze, collect, store and publish the various types of content across multiple engagement channels (to make the task easier and to optimize the return on your content investment). There are a number of relatively complete solutions for handling this, all of which can be integrated to varying degrees with each other and with your company's back-end systems.

The reality, however, is that most B2B businesses are far from such levels of optimization in the way they perform their marketing. Most don't stretch beyond conventional printed materials such as product brochures or dryly presented information—often published to their own websites in some sort of list format. For such companies, a high-end CMS would only make it possible to distribute boring information more quickly.

So while it is, of course, important to keep an eye on the future, we suggest that most B2B companies should largely ignore advanced content management solutions and concentrate on breathing life into their content first—making a difference here and now with a few well-implemented steps toward a comprehensive strategy focused on creating engaging content.

The vital importance of engaging content

Why is an engaging content strategy likely to be the single most important factor in the success of your B2B marketing and communication efforts?

Put yourself in the shoes of today's B2B buyer. Now imagine you need to buy a product you've never bought before—or you want to see if there's a better product on the market than the one you have been using. How do you discover, learn about and evaluate the product choices presented by competing manufacturers? Most of the time, you'll start with the Internet. Perhaps it's Google, perhaps your favorite industry news site. What will catch your attention? An interesting article, video or perhaps even an ad. Which of these will be most persuasive? Information presented in a clear, interesting, even entertaining way. And information which you perceive to be least biased—preferably created by one of your industry peers or, for example, an analyst whose opinion is widely respected.

Content about and around your offerings is not a nice-to-have or an additional feature of being a customer of your company. Instead, you should think of it as being every bit as important as your best-selling product or service. And, just as you wouldn't bring your products or services to market without a strategy, you need to have an equally well-considered plan and production process for the production and delivery of content that engages effectively with your target markets.

Why B2B organizations develop content

What exactly do you expect to achieve from your content development efforts? Take inspiration from those B2B marketers already in that position, and note their expectations as a result of their content programs:

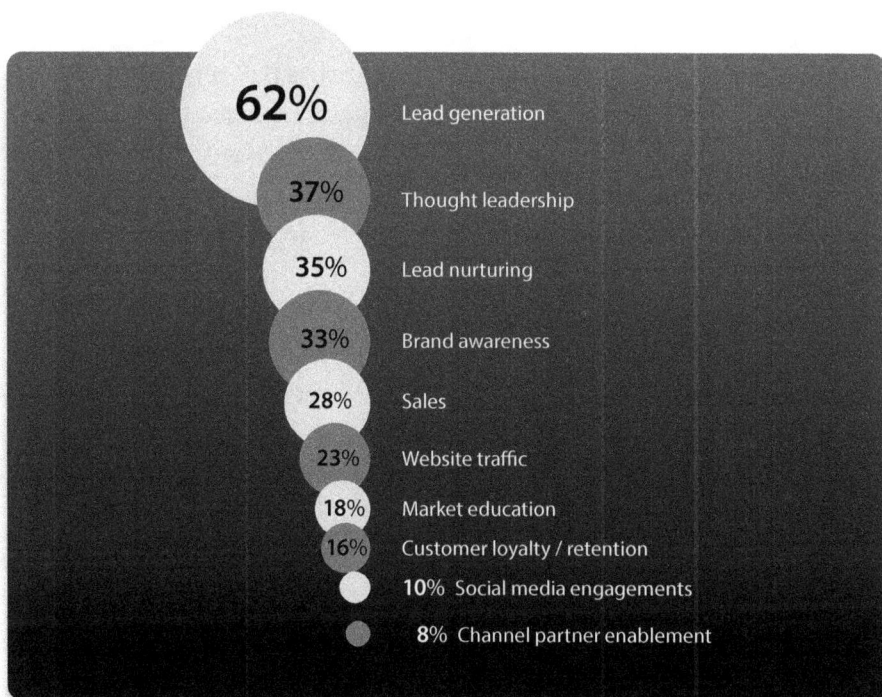

62% Lead generation

37% Thought leadership

35% Lead nurturing

33% Brand awareness

28% Sales

23% Website traffic

18% Market education

16% Customer loyalty / retention

10% Social media engagements

8% Channel partner enablement

Source: 2011 Content Marketing Trends survey of B2B Technology Marketing Community on LinkedIn

FIGURE 5.1 What marketers expect from their content development efforts.

You'll note that the top objective of B2B marketers is lead generation—they expect to build relationships with B2B prospects through their content creation which then turn into possible sales. That's a reasonable expectation—but the process will seldom be immediate.

Types of content

According to research conducted in 2011 by the 20,000 member B2B Technology Marketing Community, coming up with truly engaging content is the biggest challenge for companies who have realized the importance of content-based engagement.

What kinds of content should you plan to produce in a B2B context? In addition to the usual corporate, product and service information you have most likely been producing to date, you need a variety of different types of content. Some of it your organization can produce, some will be produced by external journalists or agencies, and some must be sourced from industry experts and other independent voices beyond your company. It's all designed to demonstrate your expertise—not via boastful statements, but through the quality of the insights, know-how, opinions and resources you make available, the stories you share and the people who are seen to be engaged with your company.

Your focus should be on meeting the needs of prospects at each of the diverse steps through their buying processes, while always providing great value through Voice of Industry, Voice of Customer and Voice of Company content.

Wherever possible, you should think about creating content that has a longer life span—items that can be accessed again and again, to provide value for prospective customers even over several years. Google looks kindly on useful evergreen content, and can continue to send highly qualified traffic to such resources for a very long time.

Which content tactics should you use for each Voice? Here's a possible allocation (but feel free to adjust to suit your own requirements; these suggestions aren't fixed in stone):

	Voice of Industry	Voice of Customer	Voice of Company
Social media	•	•	•
Article posting	•		•
In-person events	•	•	•
eNewsletters	•		•
Case studies			•
Blogs	•		•
White papers	•		•
Webinars	•	•	•
Print magazines	•		•
Videos	•		
Traditional media	•		•
Microsites			•
Print newsletters	•		•
Research reports	•		•
Data-driven marketing			•
Podcasts	•		
Digital magazines	•		•
Mobile			•
Virtual conferences	•	•	
eBooks	•	•	•

FIGURE 5.2 Possible content choices for each Voice.

You'll be familiar with most of the elements in Figure 5.2 (even if you haven't considered them in the context of a Three Voices™ strategy). However, some deserve further explanation and discussion—and a treatment that's rather different to the traditional methods. Let's start with an oldie but goodie: the white paper.

A new look at white papers

"What's new about white papers?" you may ask. "We've been doing them for decades." That may be true for white papers produced from the perspective of Voice of Company; but when you are building a truly engaging content strategy that also encompasses Voice of Industry, now is a good opportunity to think carefully about the types of topics you should cover with these papers. For example, where you may previously have used white papers to explain technical points about your products, you could now expand the subject matter to include industry-level commentary on such things as:

- The future of specific technologies

- The state of specific markets from your company's perspective

- Particular challenges or opportunities faced by your customers or the market in general

White papers are a fantastic way to engage people and generate high-quality leads—they typically rate at the top of the charts in terms of the number of visitor downloads from online sites. Think of all the places where you can advertise their existence, perhaps even including the white paper's contents page or a sample of the first few pages—enough to whet the appetite and have people register to receive the entire paper (and sign up for your email newsletter at the same time).

Case studies re-invented

Here's a way to take the propaganda out of case studies. Don't just tell how your company's brilliance saved the day for a customer, interlacing the story with countless references to your own products and people. Instead, write the story with little mention of who the supplier (your company) is, just focusing on communicating about a business that faces a challenge or opportunity, its priorities and strategy, the way in which a solution was identified and how it was implemented. That creates a far more trustworthy piece of content—one that is less likely to cause your readers to put up their guard or just stop reading. Then find a subtle, yet noticeable place to make a statement that this particular business achieved its results using your company's products and services. You'll find this sort of approach far better for engaging your audience and for having your customers agree to be the subject of a case study.

Turning how-to articles and videos into multimedia assets

B2B buyers often search for helpful guides to help them think about and take action on the challenges and opportunities they're facing. A half-hour search on Google can usually turn up one or more well-structured articles that provide valuable insights, checklists of issues to address, even suggestions for work flows. Many of these how-to articles are created by freelancers or small businesses who have learned to leverage the reach of the internet. Larger B2B companies are generally lagging behind in this area.

While a good white paper can go a long way towards satisfying customer needs for guidance, the classic, virally powered how-to article is a shorter affair, at times only comprising a checklist of, for example, the top ten things you need to think about when planning a new initiative. Such articles can do wonders for the perception of your company as a helpful, results-oriented business partner who helps your customers to think strategically about the issues they face.

Of course, you can also consider using video to help customers understand complex issues and processes. Why not, for example, leverage video to show prospects and customers how your products are installed and operated? For best results, don't overspend on formal, corporately correct film productions that few people would watch fully anyway. Instead, have a small film crew create authentic, over-the-shoulder or handheld videos with a largely unrehearsed commentary given by the person responsible for the product. In this manner, you should be able relatively inexpensively to produce a series of videos that covers your range of products.

It is far more effective to provide valuable and timely information and assistance to your stakeholders than it is to achieve a stiff and formal corporate video. Whatever you do, don't attempt to create such videos in-house (that can be a recipe for systematic brand damage). Instead, talk to your marketing or communications partners about creative approaches that can achieve the right look and feel.

Extending a corporate welcome to external thought leaders

Thanks to the internet and the accompanying wealth of knowledge-based sites and social networks, it's easier than ever to access the know-how of experts within and outside corporations: "Key Opinion Leaders" (KOLs). The term is borrowed from the pharmaceutical industry, where it describes a physician who influences the medical practices of his or her peers. Pharmaceutical companies do their best to engage key opinion leaders early in the drug development process to provide advocacy activity and feedback from a marketing perspective.

Such groups of highly knowledgeable, well-respected opinion leaders exist within and across all sorts of industries, and they are increasingly being listened to, and interacted with, by B2B buyers. Your opportunity is to provide a platform for industry KOLs to get involved with your company and to make the opinions of such people available to your stakeholders. There are a number of ways in which you might do this. One idea is to create a specialized area on your Voice of Industry site where you place KOLs alongside each other in an elite group. Then you can interview each person on a subject related to his or her specialist area; or you might ask a single question of the entire group in order to produce multiple perspectives on a topic of interest for your audiences.

You might also consider inviting a group of KOLs to contribute to a white paper on an issue of interest—a challenge faced by the industry, for example, or a perspective on emerging technologies. Here, a simple footnote mention of your company's involvement will suffice by way of branding, since helping KOLs to have their voices heard across the industry will turn into goodwill which you can use to generate valuable content in the future. That might in turn lead to a regular KOL appearance in your company's newsletter, for example, or an interview series that can appear in article form as well as a podcast or even video.

Enlisting KOLs can be made easier if you target not one but several opinion leaders at the same time, explaining to each that their profiles and opinions will be seen alongside other, well-respected peers in the industry. Describe your Voice of Industry platform to them and explain its independent nature, to reduce the risk that KOLs may decline to participate lest they be seen as promoting your company's interests.

Turning internal thought leaders into company ambassadors

Your employees know a lot about your industry. Their insights and perspectives can be valuable for your customers, and (if you can figure out how to extract, document and widely distribute this knowledge) such insider wisdom can be many times more effective than simply relying on one-to-one conversations between, for example, salespeople and customers.

Traditional approaches to marketing and communications have typically prevented R&D staff from having their say in public forums. As any professional communicator knows, the subject matter experts (SMEs) deep in company labs have a habit of being overly direct and "too" honest—far too authentic. But times have changed. Today's geeks are the voice of credibility, the evidence of your company's expertise, and their special capabilities can be channeled into appropriate contexts where their obvious lack of media training will only add to the magic for your audiences. That doesn't, however, mean that you should necessarily take such an approach in your more polished presentations—the contrast between corporate elegance and a straight-up geekish style can be quite appalling.

It's time to think about how to create and maximize meaningful connections between the SMEs in your company and their peers at your customers and how to connect them to other influencers in the industry. Of course, we're not advising you to open up Pandora's box and create a complex and difficult-to-control web of personal connections. Most B2B companies have one or two technically competent people who are able to bridge the gap between deep technical know-how and effective communication. Such people often have likeable, helpful personalities combined with a good understanding of what should and should not be shared with customers.

Here's one way to work within this area: start by capturing a number of videos, even as short as one or two minutes long, where your experts talk about some aspect of technology or provide other industry-based perspectives that you expect will appeal to a broad audience or perhaps just to a small niche of like-minded experts. An interview format—asking pre-arranged questions that your experts can readily answer—is perhaps the most effective method of enabling your experts to respond easily. Make these videos available in various forms around your content network (Voice of Company, Voice of Industry) as blog posts, on dedicated technology sites, on your corporate video platform, or even just on YouTube.

Generally, you should begin by working with just a few internal experts rather than many, expanding your program if and when the effort has proven its worth.

Online product brochures

Another area where such internally sourced expertise pieces can be very useful indeed: product launches and product informational pieces. While printed product brochures are and will remain useful sources of information, they're somewhat limited when it comes to form, distribution, keeping up-to-date and so on.

That's where a new breed of online product brochures is coming into play. A world away from the usual PDF of your printed brochure, these are specialized vehicles that provide all the technical specifications and benefits lists contained in your printed version, but supplement that information with video, audio, animations and links. Implemented properly, these online showcases can be viewed on all sorts of different devices, from desktop PCs to tablets and smartphones. And they make a perfect platform for your internal experts.

Imagine, for example, that you've just released a fabulous new widget that solves a key problem for your customers. It's based on a new generation of technology boasting a raft of advantages. Since you're working at the forefront of B2B marketing, you've created an *online* product brochure that describes and depicts the widget in detail. And now for the magic: included within the brochure is a video of one of the R&D engineers behind the product's development, talking about its wonderful new technology. It's not a carefully rehearsed piece read off a tele-prompter. Rather, it's an informal video where the engineer talks directly to a single, stationary camera. And it's clearly not propaganda but the real thing: access to the inspiration and hard work that's gone into developing such an exciting new product. What's more, the online brochure platform will enable your product information to easily be searched, shared, linked to and stored for later reference—none of which can be done with ease in a printed universe.

Take a deep breath—encourage customer reviews

Reviews of all kinds have become highly popular (and are a quintessential demonstration of the Voice of Customer in action). Consumers flock to online sources to check out what both experts and peers have to say about electronic goods, hotels, leasing plans, insurance, even the reputations of companies. In fact, reviewing has been a key building block in the success of sites such as Amazon and eBay.

Reviews and review-oriented sites are fast gaining ground in B2B contexts, too. When our agency recently looked to change its hosting services provider, for example, the decision was made primarily on the results of a search for B2B buyer reviews of the major players in that industry. These painted a clear and convincing picture of both our existing and prospective providers, and turned up many useful hints and tips along the way.

A 2008 study by *Christian C Carlsson* (*"Ratings and reviews for the business user"*) concluded that reviews and ratings of B2B products:

- Make it easy to sort through products by rating
- Speed up the decision process
- Increase the understanding of a product or service
- Increase trust in the manufacturer or service provider
- Help in minimizing risk
- Help in minimizing time by directly removing (those that rate poorly)

We recommend that you create review-oriented content because it can drive search traffic to the Voice of Industry site you've created and motivates visitors to share the reviews with others. Of course, your company cannot be seen to create and disseminate articles or videos that review competing products (either favorably or negatively). Instead, you should consider creating review-based content that focuses on, for example, recently released industry reports. Include your company's opinions and add a few facts to confirm or take issue with the report. Or simply create an article that reviews a new book on a subject relevant to the industry. If your company manufactures automobiles, for example, why not critically review associated products such as motor oil or tires?

You should also open up your own products and services to customer review. Of course, this risks attracting negative comments (and you need to be ready for that) but it also gives you plenty of opportunity to respond to such comments, dealing with the issues raised and perhaps addressing concerns that have been felt but not expressed by a number of other customers.

Blogger *Mike Moran* provides a useful perspective on B2B reviews:

> Manufacturers, especially those selling to businesses, have been slow to warm to reviews as a selling tool. A 2009 survey of B2B respondents showed that more than 95 percent had used consumer product reviews; but almost 40 percent had never used B2B reviews even once.
>
> It's easy to see why B2B marketers have shied away. If a potential customer reads a bad review on Amazon, they just move along and buy a different book from the site. But when someone sees a manufacturer's product being panned right on its site, they might head over to a competitor's site to buy something else. At least that's the fear.
>
> Sun Microsystems Inc. had to overcome such fears before it became one of the first B2B companies to show ratings and reviews for its products.
>
> Bad reviews that drive away customers are a real danger, but when Sun tested the idea, it found that for every bad review it gets, it gets several good ones. Curt Sasaki, vice president of Sun's web properties, approached the project believing that "the more folks that did reviews, the more it would balance out—it's self-correcting." Sun knows that its customers will look elsewhere for product reviews, so why not keep those people on Sun's website?

Being able to see how others are experiencing your products and services can, in fact, make purchasing less complex for customers, as they may learn from the experiences of others who have, for example, bought a model that was not sufficiently powerful to do the job. Knowing this could induce the potential purchaser to specify a sturdier model from your range.

Opening up to reviews also gives your company more credibility (that vital ingredient again!) and may help to safeguard against potentially damaging, angry reviews placed on other non-company-controlled platforms.

Ratings and Reviews Rev Up Results

Automobile purchase guide Cars.com provides an online marketplace for vehicle advertisers. The company's site is visited by over 10 million auto enthusiasts and potential buyers each month.

The company discovered that web pages that enabled ratings and reviews resulted in 16 percent higher lead conversions and 100 percent more traffic clicking through to auto dealer sites. For visits that included customer reviews, 45 percent more visitors clicked through to the company's automobile finance calculator compared with those who did not read reviews, perhaps indicating greater intent to buy.

Source: www.bazaarvoice.com

Leveraging industry news as a traffic magnet

B2B companies have traditionally created a steady stream of press releases, usually published on their own websites. At worst, such press releases are pure propaganda; at best they can be somewhat uninspiring, perhaps because they are typically written from the company's own perspective, recounting deals recently won or incremental product improvements.

Thinking "news items" in a Three Voices™ perspective encourages us to focus on a broader range of items: some about the company's own endeavors, many others about happenings in the industry as a whole.

You might imagine a future scenario where industry stakeholders of all kinds flock to your Voice of Industry site to pick up their daily ration of top news items. (There are, of course, already excellent sites that do this today for specific industries, such as www.foodnavigator.com for the food industry). If your company were able to direct which news items were emphasized (making sure that stories which supported your own views were appropriately prioritized) and could examine the behavior of those viewing the various articles and videos, you would gain a significant advantage over your competitors. But where can you source such news? To what extent can you simply re-publish items or do you need to re-write and even add perspectives to items you've found?

Reality check: the idea of creating a newsroom complete with an editor, journalists and all the other elements that it takes to drive a site capable of locating and releasing news in a timely fashion is far, far beyond most B2B companies. For the few that can do it, it is a major investment.

One such company is technology provider Cisco, which released its technology news site (a blend of Voice of Company and Voice of Industry), in June 2011. Located at newsroom.cisco.com, the comprehensive site's aim is to lead news dissemination and steer topical issues for Cisco's business, market segments and its many partners.

"The Network" reflects the company's involvement in the networking equipment industry and features categories such as Data Center, Collaboration, Video, Social Media, Core Networks and the rather company-centric Cisco Culture. Viewers can sort news items by date or topic via an All News tab. Cisco has also been careful to make sure its content can be integrated with key social media tools such as Facebook or Twitter, allowing easy shareability.

Corporate statements about how Cisco planned to handle content and engagement with the site are interesting to examine. Each of the topics mentioned above is assigned a "page manager" who is responsible for providing a steady flow of compelling content that delivers on the site's mission. From the outset, the site's content was contributed by a small group comprising both internal Cisco staff and well-known external industry figures such as Steve Wildstrom of BusinessWeek, Mark Gunther of Fortune magazine, and John Carey (an independent writer who has covered hi-tech industries for more than thirty years). Today, the site is fed by a far wider variety of content sources and demonstrates best practices in the company newsroom field.

Even for companies of Cisco's size, setting up and running a news site is no small task. It demands clear objectives from the outset, as well as careful planning, a budget large enough to handle in-house or outsourced content creation, and the backing of top management.

Embrace controversy

"Don't rock the boat" seems to be an unshakeable rule in many companies. Strangely enough, companies who adhere to the status quo are often the ones to be left behind when the boat is rocking at industry level. Ask Nokia or Sony Ericsson, for example, why Apple was able to not just rock but almost overturn their boats.

Dissenting opinion drives our world forward, and both boat-rockers and those who prefer to sit quietly are attracted in some way or other by ideas that are in conflict with the status quo. It gets their attention and gets them personally involved at various levels. But B2B companies are typically reluctant to publish any opinions that might be in conflict with what any of their stakeholders think.

Here's our recommendation: become a company with an opinion. But first, identify the kinds of topics you should have an opinion about, who should express that opinion and in what tone and style. Then get busy writing, for example, an article with your CEO as author about the company's opinion on proposed new legislation—or take a contrarian view on a recently released industry report or prominent blog post. Use the debates that may be raging in your industry to express a strong opinion, but ensure it emerges from high enough up in the organization to be properly aligned with the values of your company.

Turn events from distractions to the main attraction

Few B2B organizations have capitalized on the full potential of the events they regularly hold for prospects, customers and business partners. Typically the focus is on sending out invitations via one or two email shots, getting people to register for the event, then turning attention to ensuring the event delivers what it should on the day.

The changing world of the B2B buyer has turned events thinking upside down.

Now the lead-up period to each event, and post-event activities that leverage and build upon what is presented on the day, have become every bit as important as the event itself.

Platforms put in place to support your Three Voices™ strategy will enable you to begin highlighting the theme of the event months beforehand, generating interest among those who follow your Voice of Industry articles. Among the registered or unregistered visitors to your Voice of Industry activities, you can solicit early expressions of interest, using these to figure out whether your theme is on target and indicating what your audience sees as the most important aspects of the event.

Following each event, you can ask for feedback, distribute presentations and seed discussions about points raised by speakers. You will usually notice, too, a flurry of activity following each event as people start connecting with each other and with individual speakers. Such connections are, of course, encouraged and supplemented through networking breaks during the events themselves.

A good Three Voices™ strategy, then, incorporates events at its core, using them to strengthen the bonds between the company and buyers, as well as between buyers. It comprises both offline and online events, sometimes simultaneously (as in the case of an event held in one city but relayed to other centers via the web).

If your company is typical of B2B companies around the world, you're probably already running periodic, seminar-style events in the physical world. But you are unlikely to be maximizing these events from pre- and post-event perspectives. And we suspect you won't be far down the track of setting up webinars or other online events in ways that extract the full potential of such activities. If you are doing this, give yourself a pat on the back—you're well on the way to exploiting the power of a Three Voices™ strategy!

Unveil new insights with your own survey reports

It's hard to think of a more powerful form of lead-generating content than a report based on a survey.

Perhaps that's because there's something B2B buyers seek before they choose a product or service: insights driven by the wisdom of the crowd. The more knowledge a prospective purchaser feels he has about the type of solution being considered, and the more he knows about the experiences of peers who have acted before him, the more comfortable he will be.

You can bring incredible perceived value to your customers by providing them with such insights. Keep these insights factual and objective, making your company more credible and trustworthy.

Research reports firmly establish your company as a thought leader—thinking beyond its own horizons in an attempt to uncover what the market really thinks, how it behaves, and exactly what it wants. With today's low-cost, cloud-based solutions for running systematic surveys (we've used www.surveymonkey. com with success, but there are many more out there), you can easily set up and distribute an online questionnaire that forms the basis of a survey report.

Unless research is your core business, you should make your survey reports free of charge and distribute them as widely as you can. Take the time to produce a properly designed set of questions, because this will help avoid answers that are too varied or unreliable to be reported in a well-structured way. There are plenty of how-to guides on the web to help you work your way through the possible pitfalls of questionnaire design.

Engaging content

It's time to take a closer look at exactly how we might be able to engage our customers through content. Here's a collection of topic suggestions (adapted from a blog post by *Mark Brownlow*, with additional material from the white paper *"Facebook's EdgeRank: how to make sure you're in the news feed"* by *Buddy Media*):

1. **Ask questions**
   Perhaps the most effective way to engage with your customers and prospects is simply by posting questions. People love to talk about themselves and offer their thoughts—sometimes even when you don't ask for it.

   Ask about their needs, their wants and their most pressing issues— and encourage your readers to share personal stories related to your product or service category. This can serve as an excellent tool to increase interaction, as the conversation may even encourage your followers to talk to each other. Your goal should be to publish questions that your audience will want to answer and share.

2. **Join conversations already in progress**
   The ability to keep a conversation going should be a large part of your publishing strategy. This means that when people write comments on your articles or post their own content, your brand should contribute to the discussion to maintain user engagement.

   Some brands find that even corresponding with what some people call "trolls" (those who make unhelpful or negative comments) can be an extremely effective way to boost your engagement. Let's face it, not all content that is posted is positive, yet brands can take advantage of this dilemma to put out fires and increase the number of engagements on a topic.

   People love to see how brands interact with customers, so regardless of whether or not the content posted is positive, basic curiosity will draw readers to the conversation.

3. **Be topical**
   Wherever you can, find a way to relate your content to current news, events and trends, and post questions or state your position.

   By asking people what they think about breaking news or other hot topics, organizations can encourage conversations that have been known to generate impressive amounts of traffic.

4. **Share problems and solutions**
   Identify common problems faced by your readership and suggest some solutions. If you're publishing through your Voice of Industry channels, don't make this self-serving by always conveniently finding problems that can only be solved with your own paid expertise or product. Self-promotion is fine, but not if it's at the expense of delivering value.

5. **Give how-tos**
   Create a video or write a guide on how best to undertake a particular task or use a particular product or service. Again, make the solution supplier-agnostic when in Voice of Industry mode.

6. **Top tips**
   Produce a series of tips that help people do their job better or get more out of products and services in your category, or anything else in which readers are likely to share an interest.

7. **Opinion/analysis**
   Offer a considered analysis or subjective opinion on a relevant topic, idea, event, news item, product, company, industry development, performance, etc. that's of importance to your audience.

8. **Look into the future**
   Write an article predicting the future of your sector. Some time later, write a follow-up examining whether you were right or not (and if you were wrong, why?)

9. **Fable**
   Take a leaf out of Aesop's book and report on a story or news item apparently irrelevant to your context. Then draw out a parallel to a relevant business situation or issue. Or a lesson that readers can apply to their own situation.

10. **Horror/disaster story**
    Write about a difficult or disastrous business experience or decision, and use it to draw out lessons for other relevant business situations. Most audiences love to read about other people's problems and how they dealt with them.

11. **Reviews**
    Consider reviewing other people's products and services. No, not the competition (there may be a suggestion of bias in your comments). Review useful tools, books and similar items of benefit to your audience, but which aren't competing with your own offerings.

12. **"Best of"**
    Look back at what proved most popular with readers in the past and consider producing a "best of" summary every now and then. Don't overdo it, as people will inevitably tire of repeated content.

    Timeless material produced early on in your content creation program probably reached a mere fraction of your current readership. Dig a little into the subscriber numbers and subscription lengths and you might find a wealth of material that's effectively new to the majority of the recipients.

    "Best of" content also makes a great solution in an emergency… when you're stuck for content.

13. **Surveys/feedback requests**
    Another highly engaging feature is the reader survey or a request for specific feedback. You might do this to give readers a welcome chance to help guide the future direction of your content program. Or you can ask them for opinions or feedback on other topics.

    Of course, the results of such a survey are themselves valuable content for another issue. Consider surveying technical staff in your industry on the main problems they face in their jobs, then summarize the answers in an article a couple of issues later.

14. **Event recommendations**

    Point people to useful events both online and offline: webinars, conferences, workshops and so on. They might be directly related to your industry or (even better) only tangentially related but focused on skills and expertise that translate handily to your sector.

15. **Resource links**

    Nearly everyone has difficulty finding time to stay up to date with what's going on beyond the immediate environment. So sifting through the online morass to pick out the most useful links is a service everyone appreciates.

    Direct your readers to third-party websites, articles, online tools and similar you think they are likely to appreciate, ideally with a short explanation of why you think these resources are worth noting.

16. **Answering feedback**

    Consider creating a dedicated section for answering reader questions. This is a great way to kick-start your creativity, give you a chance to demonstrate expertise and show readers you're actually listening.

17. **Crowd-sourced**

    Even without creating a full-blown forum or community website, you can encourage audience-sourced contributions.

18. **Interviews**

    Interviews make great content. It's like picking a topic and getting someone else to write the article. You can interview people from within your organization, a reader, a customer or an expert in some related aspect of business.

    Don't underestimate the effort you need to put in. Considered thought needs to go into the choice of interview partner, the interview topic and the questions themselves. And if the interview is oral, you'll need time to transcribe and edit the recording.

19. **News**

    Reporting relevant industry news is safe, but unlikely to be a genre-busting home run in terms of establishing your content as a unique read. Unless of course, you do it very well indeed.

20. **Statistics and lists**
    Take a look at any media site publishing practical articles and
    the most popular pages usually carry titles like "Top 5 ways…",
    "Ten tips for…", "Seven steps to… ".

    People like numbers and people like lists, for example:

    - Top 10 challenges faced by IT staff

    - Top five reasons to change jobs NOW

    - Top 5 email clients for your mobile phone

    Benchmarking and industry statistics always go down well,
    particularly if you can aggregate numbers from various sources,
    saving people the time and effort of doing so themselves.

21. **Give a call to action**
    Use your posts to tell people exactly what you want them to do. In
    many cases, publishing content that you think might generate traffic
    isn't always enough. Be explicit and publish call-outs that will explain
    to your users exactly what action you want them to take.

Of course, none of these suggestions are mutually exclusive—mix and match
different types of content to deliver the kind of engaging material that resonates
best with your audience.

Making your content remarkable

Even if you follow all the content suggestions we've featured thus far, there's
one more hurdle to be overcome: ensuring that your content is worth reading
(and, ideally, worth sharing).

Here's a checklist of some twenty attributes (some of which we've drawn from
Tippit's white paper on the topic) that can make your content more memorable,
impactful, and effective—in other words, remarkable.

WHAT MAKES CONTENT REMARKABLE?

1. Your message needs to be **relevant** to your audience—and to their audiences as well, if you want the content to be shared beyond the initial recipients.

2. It needs to be **fresh**—stale news won't get past the Delete key.

3. Your news needs to be **worth buzzing about.**

4. Your news needs to be **exclusive**—those potentially sharing the information want to be seen as "in the know", ahead of the pack.

5. There should be an element of **scarcity** involved to drive urgency ("only 150 made", "only until [date]").

6. It needs to come from a **credible** source.

7. The focus of your message needs to be **the right stuff** (i.e. a product or project worthy of our attention).

8. **Helpful**—Does your content help solve problems? "Always be helping" is the new "always be closing".

9. **Timely**—Is this a story that breaks new ground rather than a retread?

10. **Targeted**—Is the content intended to inform those "just looking", "close to buying" or in the post-purchase phase?

11. **Interruptive**—Is there a captivating element that grabs and sustains attention?

12. **Entertaining**—Is there a novel or enjoyable aspect that is well-conceived and engaging?

13. **Illuminating**—will it lead to "Aha!" moments for recipients?

14. **Shareable**—Does it have a viral quality? Would an influencer want to forward it, or post it?

15. **Progressive**—Is there a call to action or next step?

16. **Versatile**—Can it be leveraged across media channels?

17. **Crowd-sourced**—Does it involve customers or partners in the spirit of cooperation?

18. **Efficient**—Is it concise, perhaps in an effective list format, to offset diminished attention spans online?

19. **Attractive**—is it graphically interesting and will it stand out?

20. **Integrated**—Does it fit with your existing or upcoming communications?

Once you've subjected your content to all these exacting specifications (and it's still surviving), it's time for our next stop: identifying how this carefully crafted material can best be distributed.

Key take-outs

- A Three Voices™ strategy enables meaningful engagement between the company, its customers and prospects, and other stakeholders.

- Effective engagement requires a content strategy that describes the what, why, how, for whom, by whom, with what, when, where, how often, what next and measurement issues around your content.

- As we all become more online and more socially connected online, more of our conversations are public.

- Information should be presented in a clear, interesting, even entertaining way.

- A variety of different types of content demonstrates your B2B company's expertise via the quality of the insights, know-how, opinions and sources you make available, the stories you share and the people who are seen to be engaged with your company.

- Prioritize opinionated, original content that has a longer life span and provides value for prospective customers.

- Supplement printed information with different content formats such as video, audio, animations and links.

- Reviews and review-oriented sites are fast gaining ground in B2B contexts, and their use can add to your company's credibility.

- Encourage both positive and negative customer reviews, creating review-oriented content that can drive search traffic to your Voice of Industry site and motivate visitors to share the reviews with others.

- Unveil new insights with your own survey reports, demonstrating that your company thinks beyond its own horizon.

Notes

CHAPTER SIX:

Delivering content for the three Voices

Particularly relevant types of media

There are many different media, both online and offline, established and emerging, that B2B businesses can use to address their audiences. We don't intend to provide a complete run-down of all the various media choices you could make to engage with stakeholders, but there are a number of useful yet often under-utilized media that make particular sense to deploy in relation to your Voice of Industry, Voice of Company and Voice of Customer activities. Let's review some of these media choices:

Blogs

Merriam-Webster's online dictionary defines a blog (originally "web log") as: a web site that contains an online personal journal with reflections, comments, and often hyperlinks provided by the writer; also: the contents of such a site. According to NM Incite, a Nielsen/McKinsey company, more than 181 million public blogs were in existence by 2011.

B2B companies have had mixed experiences with blogs. In fact, we've seen countless blog deaths among our B2B clients. These unfortunate blogs were often started by enthusiastic marketing departments keen to display a vibrant corporate culture—a more human side of the company—to stakeholders in an attempt to build trust and engagement. That's a great aim, but there are many challenges and pitfalls when using blogging in business contexts.

So what types of business blogs are really effective? First and foremost, blogs that work are generally created by a single, highly motivated blogger, not as a result of a strategic decision by a corporation with thousands of employees. Understanding this is key to developing blogs that will survive past the initial few months of existence.

If there's one thing we've learned over the years about blogging, it's this: blogging is best done by bloggers. In other words, if you have people within your company who love to write and enjoy communicating with others across the web, then you have a real chance of creating and maintaining a thriving blog. If not, if you construct a blog and then attempt to encourage, threaten or otherwise motivate your employees to write comments with any reasonable frequency, you will likely fail.

Another key point is that blogs have to be about something. Most people have encountered blogs whose owners view them as places to dump all sorts of different ideas, impressions, references and so on without a particular theme. This is, of course, a recipe for disaster, as readers or viewers of blogs connect best with those that have a singular purpose or topic area.

So don't go setting up a blog that is just "our company's blog". Instead, find out who in your company would like to write a blog or who may consent to appearing in a video blog, and establish what he or she would like to (and is able to) cover. Then figure out how that person's urge to communicate can be turned to your company's advantage (in line with your business strategy) and give your would-be blogger all the support he or she needs to get things off the ground.

Don't forget to identify what value this new blog should bring to a specific audience. Define its mission in life. Give it a clear verbal and visual personality consistent with the company's style and personality. But also encourage your blogger to bring his or her own personality quirks to the table (as long as they're not too off-beat, of course).

Treat each new blog as an experiment. Don't expend vast resources planning and setting up the ultimate solution, then launching it in a tidal wave of promotional messages to all your stakeholders. Just set up a basic content management and publishing system and encourage your would-be blogger to begin shaping ideas and writing the first articles. Help him or her to work out the blog's editorial mission and provide constructive feedback from the company's point of view.

While you're doing this, remember the old adage that trying to add five percent more value to a project can remove fifty percent of the employee's motivation. This applies particularly strongly to blogging, where it is crucial that the blog owner's personal priorities, ideas and style consistently make themselves felt. Ignore these aspects and you'll likely be left holding the baby as your disgruntled blogger beats a hasty retreat.

Most likely, however, you will be able to find an employee or two keen to take on the responsibility of building and maintaining a blog—at least in terms of creating content and building a community. Make it clear to them that they have a greater level of freedom than through other forms of corporate communication, but that the blog is, in essence, a corporate platform rather than their own personal soap box. As such, each blog will require a document that spells out the reasons for its existence and a set of guidelines that cover what is and what is not considered good blogging, both from general social networking practices and from a corporate perspective (your Social Media Guidelines).

Also make clear to your employee bloggers the context in which they'll be expected to blog. Voice of Industry bloggers will be expected to wax lyrical about the category in general, whilst Voice of Company bloggers will be much more focused on the goings-on at your organization (although in a manner that's not overtly commercial).

Blogs, in particular, can create large followings for their authors—so you might find yourself in an unfortunate situation where you have helped a key employee to build their blog platform and accumulate hundreds or even thousands of followers, only to have them leave the company and take almost all of this carefully nurtured audience with them. That's show business, folks—at least in today's world. You can indeed lose the investment you've made—although if the blogger's new employers don't have the same perspective on the importance of propaganda-free communications, you might find your audiences slipping back to you after being hit over the head one too many times with a blatant sales pitch.

On the other hand, you may be the one luring well-followed bloggers into your organization. Give careful thought to the implications if you encourage them to continue their blogging under your banner. Bringing such people into the corporate fold may be risky, but there are also significant marketing rewards.

In our experience, people who have established successful blogs are highly aware of their own abilities and "market price", and this may have implications for how they can be successfully integrated within your company. You'll also need to consider the possible subscriber fallout if your corporate blogging philosophies are significantly at odds with what these bloggers have been covering in the past.

Podcasts

Podcasts have been around for several years now, but it's only recently that mainstream B2B marketers and communicators have begun to get interested in them as a unique vehicle for reaching audiences in situations that were previously difficult or impossible. After all, how many ways are there to deliver a one-hour presentation to someone working out on a Sunday morning at the gym? Or to present a case study to a commuter jammed into a subway train at 6 p.m.? Driving, exercising, commuting, cooking, cleaning—thanks to podcasting technology, these have all become opportunities for marketers to reach their audiences with in-depth messages. Work/life balance is, after all, an individual choice!

Properly executed business podcasts can build a recurring audience—a loyal following that will listen closely to what you have to say, often in a completely uninterrupted flow.

So what does it take to produce a podcast? First, think about your podcasts in the context of a radio or TV talk show. Each show has its own, carefully tailored concept with a clear editorial mission. You'll need to decide up front whether yours is a Voice of Industry show (with light commercial branding to indicate that your organization is the sponsor) or whether you can use the airtime as a Voice of Company affair to deal specifically with your products—in which case, what you gain in commercialization you're likely to lose in listeners. Whatever you decide, be consistent in subsequent episodes.

Shows are usually broadcast with a planned regularity. There's a consistent host who either delivers the entire show or interviews other people. Each show follows a consistent format. For podcasts, there's generally a brief introduction sequence, including music and a standard statement such as "Welcome to the

Burger Heaven podcast—a series that discusses the latest tastes and textures of the burgers you most like to eat." There's often background music that fades in and out at appropriate transition points in the content. You will also need to design a standard graphical image to act as the "masthead" for each show. All of these elements help to brand your podcast and make it stand out from other, competing podcasts in online podcast directories.

Research has shown that audiences tend to judge the quality of podcasts not just on their content and the presentation skills of the host, but also on a key aspect of production: sound quality. All too many podcasts distract and frustrate their listeners with poor room acoustics, or peripheral noises that constantly steal the listener's valuable attention. So you need to invest in the right equipment and recording environment to achieve sound quality that creates a warm, clear experience—with little or no background noise. That means thinking carefully about where and how you record, and investing in a good microphone. There are a variety of microphones available, and different types are designed for different situations. Choose one that suits your recording environment and remember to conduct an audio test to check sound quality and background noise before each recording session.

There are other parameters that make a difference to the listening experience such as the distance between the person speaking and the microphone (consider using a microphone/headset combination to ensure a consistent distance), or simply the amount of warmth and enthusiasm in the presenter's voice! It's also important to record your podcasts in the same environment each time, to ensure a consistent listening experience that, over time, becomes part of your podcast's unique brand.

With the recording completed, you may want to run some basic editing software to reduce defects and errors. You can use the same software to remove long pauses or undesirable noises that may have intruded while the show was being recorded.

In the final analysis, podcasting is about bringing attention to yourself and your business. It may not result in direct sales, but it can help you build a relationship with prospects and customers and boost trust in your company. For best results, contact someone with real-world podcasting expertise to help you determine and set up the best podcasting solution so you can get off to a good start from the very first broadcast.

Webinars

A "webinar" (a short form of "web-based seminar") is a lecture, presentation, seminar or workshop transmitted over the internet by one or more presenters or panelists to a large audience at a scheduled time. Properly planned and implemented webinars can represent a valuable asset for B2B marketers. Of course, as with any new communication form, webinars can negatively affect your brand, too. Here's what professional blogger and disillusioned participant Erik Deckers had to say about his experience with webinars he had attended:

> "They were all death on a stick. PowerPoint presentations, facilitators
> read the script, and interaction was nothing more than a quick poll.
> I think my time would have been better spent reading an article
> about the same topic."

These are words of warning—not to avoid this form of event as an element of the B2B marketing mix, but to give webinars the attention they deserve and the effort required to get it right.

Unlike webcasts, which are simply one-way broadcast events that are often pre-recorded, the emphasis with webinars should be on audience participation, including polling and question and answer sessions. Information is presented on-screen, with the presenter speaking over a teleconferenced phone line or Voice-over-IP communication via the computer itself. Webinars require specialized internet-based technologies available from many different suppliers, typically incorporating email and calendar functions to enable event setup as well as two-way dialogue during the event.

Lasting as long as an hour (sometimes two), webinars are particularly relevant in B2B contexts where products are often technically complex and difficult to describe in a simple product brochure. The beauty of a webinar lies in the way it enables representatives from your company (and/or external experts you have engaged) to address large, geographically dispersed audiences with the kind of presentations typically reserved for physical company-to-customer meetings or rare speaking engagements at industry conferences. If you include an online discussion forum at the end of the session, your audience will be able to provide valuable feedback and ideas for everything from product development to promotional approaches.

Most of the B2B companies we talk to recognize the benefits of webinars—particularly given the valuable market feedback they can provide. Webinars help companies to reach audiences that may have difficulty attending meetings or conferences (e.g. one-person departments that find it hard to leave the office). But they can have mixed results—and the difference is in their design and delivery and the degree of engagement allowed.

Generally speaking, the success of B2B webinars is directly linked to the level of interactivity provided during the session. A webinar that takes the form of a lecture-style presentation doesn't take into account that many in the audience are, in fact, multi-tasking while they participate. They're more likely to tune in when they can get some hands-on learning, follow a relevant case study or hear the opinions of their peers.

For advice on running effective and engaging webinars, we turned to an expert. *Julia Young* of web meeting software developers *Facilitate.com* shares these helpful insights:

1. **Design your agenda with a distracted participant in mind.**
   Assume that participants will be multi-tasking unless you keep them fully engaged. Be sure to design your agenda with:

   - Tight content

   - Lively speakers

   - No more than 10 minutes or 3 slides of talking before a fully interactive exercise

   - More than 50% of the total webinar time spent collecting and responding to ideas, questions and perspectives from participants

2. **Give out slides in advance—review briefly and then start asking provocative questions.** We learn more from engaging with ideas than by sitting and listening to a 45-minute presentation (while checking our email). People like to make notes, mark up interesting points and add their own ideas. So send out your slides in advance, cut your presentation time to a minimum and start asking and answering questions of your participants. A slide-only presentation is as passive as the TV.

3. **Skip the video—prepare for a good dialogue between a moderator and expert.** Use video as a way to attract people to your webinar and give them an introduction before you start—skip it during the real-time event. In many cases, video adds an unnecessary level of complexity and often isn't done well. Instead, spend your preparation time to create a rich dialogue between a moderator and your subject matter expert.

4. **Don't compromise the interactive learning portion of your workshop.** Seek out web meeting tools designed to pull information in from participants rather than just pushing information out. If you would use sticky notes and flip charts in a face-to-face session, then look for similar tools for your online session. Keep the technology simple and only use what will really add value.

5. **Steal ideas from others.**
   Take some time to participate in different webinars to see how others are doing it. Make notes as to what works and what doesn't—when are you engaged and when are you distracted? Copy the best examples shamelessly.

6. **Look for ways to engage your participants before the webinar.**
   Whether designing a webinar for marketing purposes, to extend the reach of your expertise or delivering corporate training, don't limit your engagement with participants to the 60-90 minute teleconference. Send out a survey; provide an online space for introductions; ask participants for their questions ahead of time. Knowing your audience and why they are taking the time to attend will allow you to focus the webinar content and tailor your interaction.

7. **Follow-up after the webinar.**
   Follow up afterwards by providing an ongoing forum for additional ideas and reflections; keep the conversation going around a focused set of questions. This gives participants time to apply the learning, share their experiences and keep coming back for more.

Last but not least, master the technology—practice your webinar skills well in advance to avoid souring the experience due to technical glitches while your audience waits.

As you might expect, B2B webinars benefit from careful planning—not just on the logistics side of things. To begin with, you should seek professional advice to help you build a compelling concept around the event. Determine a name, design a logo and tagline, think about visual elements, tone and style. Spend as much time as is necessary to put together an effective strategy for attracting the maximum number of participants. Plan to record your webinars as well, enabling the event to reach those who couldn't attend.

While this may seem like a lot of work, the extra effort will boost the success of your webinars, increasing the number of participant sign-ups and enabling you to turn what might have been a one-off success into a regular series of events highly valued and well attended by prospects and customers.

Videos

As we've stressed earlier, content is the key driver for audience engagement. When we go online we are looking for things that entertain or inform us, or both. If it is compelling and relevant it doesn't matter whether a big name studio, an enthusiastic amateur or a brand created it. And because so many people and enterprises are developing new and innovative ways to talk to other people, tell stories and distinguish themselves, we are seeing some remarkable innovations in what is being done with the medium of video. These developments are occurring in the forms videos take, the technologies that deliver them and the way that people interact with them.

Web users seem to have an unquenchable thirst for video. In fact, a 2010 Cisco VNI Forecast report asserted that, by 2014, more than 90 percent of all web traffic will be video—with more than one billion video users worldwide and data traffic four times that of 2010.

But is video a relevant medium for reaching and persuading B2B buyers? Video content has been shown to lead to deeper engagement with audiences. And it can have a number of additional positive impacts across other digital channels. In 2009, Nate Elliot of Forrester Research, Inc. reported that video was approximately 53 times more likely than traditional text-heavy web pages to appear on the first page of search results. Put simply, according to Nate's findings, videos had a one in 11,000 chance of landing on the first page of Google results, while text-based pages have something like a one in 500,000 chance. Whether you agree with Forrester's methodology or not (and some have raised questions as to its validity), it seems clear that video integration can drive SEO value to a significant extent, most likely for B2B audiences, too.

However you interpret such data, the point is that video has become a very compelling and very mainstream offering, particularly on the web. And that makes video content a critical marketing priority.

There's just one problem. The B2B market is ready for video, but B2B marketing and communication budgets are typically not. Making videos in corporate contexts has never been an easy and inexpensive task. Perhaps for this reason, many companies in the B2B space have limited their production rate to between two and five videos per year. Usually, the topic of such videos has been a (hopefully) brief presentation about either the company or a new product. Some have created customer testimonials or themed videos about the company's product design approach. But that's usually where it stops—along with the funding that would be required to deploy video more widely. With the current acceleration in the use of video as a competitive B2B tool, however, and with budgets allocated at least a year ahead, marketing and communication managers need to quickly enlighten top management about the growing importance of this medium.

But surely videos nowadays can be created much more cheaply? The answer is yes. Yes, that is, in relation to a couple of decades ago before the arrival of powerful editing and animation software. But since then, nothing much has changed on the pricing front. There are several reasons for this. Probably the most important factor is that the basic process has not, and most likely cannot be, changed. It still takes just as much time and money to figure out the story you want to tell with your video, the way in which the storyline will unfold, the cinematic effects that will be used and the strategy behind the completed video's delivery. There are other elements, too, such as the all-important, consistent branding elements that appear at the beginning and end of each video you create. In the vast majority of cases, the services of a creative agency and film production team are still required to arrive at a polished result that can make itself stand out amongst a fast-growing number of videos clamoring for audience attention.

But isn't it possible to use an iPhone or Peter from R&D's digital SLR Canon to create short videos with that from-the-hip, down-to-earth, authentically genuine feeling? Isn't that the sort of stuff that will give us street credibility?

Sometimes, you may get lucky. That one-minute, hand-held camera or mobile phone footage you grabbed while your European vice president of sales was in your office may turn out to look like a convincing, creative piece of work (although admittedly, the sound quality could have been better). But continuing to work in this way will produce another twenty videos of unusable quality, as well as many wasted opportunities to capture a great piece of content, before you decide to call in a professional team.

We'd like to take a moment to issue a plea to B2B companies around the world: please don't create another in-house produced video where one of your product development engineers stands stiffly and uncomfortably in front of a single, fixed-angle camera, struggling with a rehearsed or tele-prompted script. It's not going to make your company look like a leader in its field. More likely, you will appear clumsy and unprofessional, and the presentation's lack of quality may lead viewers to question the overall quality of your products or services.

Some companies that have realized the importance of video early on have taken steps to set up an in-house studio with the right backdrops and sound equipment to enable consistently high quality video productions. A number have even contracted the regular services of a professional host/interviewer to deliver that professional touch and feel on-camera.

These brands have recognized that, on the web, anyone can be a content publisher and distributor and they've taken a pragmatic approach to video. They are utilizing it to tell stories, open up dialogue and create consistent online brand identities across the multiple platforms that people are using.

An in-house studio approach is great for specific contexts, such as interviews or webinar presentations and, if you have the space and can swing the budget, we highly recommend it. You will still, however, require careful planning, a good storyboard and at least one person with extensive film-making experience to obtain results that will consistently support rather than endanger your brand.

We often hear people talk about the web as allowing true democratization of media and distribution. Even so, creating engaging and successful video content and then extracting maximum value from that content is a challenging enterprise. Formats can range from creative and conceptual—pushing subtle or overt brand messaging in the form of webisodes and short documentaries—through to functional and specific, with demonstration videos showing product benefits in a very engaging manner and armed with testimonials from happy customers.

Here's a list of common applications for video:

- Brand channel—create a company "TV channel"
- Advertising—ad-style commercials
- Customer testimonials and reviews
- Education—training, seminars, guidelines
- Innovation—new products and services based on video
- Campaigns—marketing campaigns, user-generated content, competitions

Video is more engaging, more interactive and more personal than most other forms of content. As a result, it provides significant gains across fundamentals such as brand awareness and consideration, as well as increases in more direct revenue measures. Video content should be deployed to answer specific business challenges, becoming an integral part of a clear communication strategy with clear objectives. B2B marketers and communicators should begin to ask themselves where video fits into their communication planning—what is the company's video strategy?

GUERRILLA VIDEO TIPS FOR RAPID DEPLOYMENT

In this age of YouTube, not every video needs to be a corporate epic. *Jeffrey Gitomer* offers up some quick video content tips in his book *"Social Boom!"*:

- Create a library of customer testimonials, tips and ideas about your product that appear in no brochure.

- Record business philosophies that you have and want to share with others.

- Record your best idea of the week.

- Record your favorite customer of the week.

And *Wayne Wall* of video marketing specialists *Flimp Media* tosses his own tips into the mix:

- Keep it short: Your video should be 2 or 3 minutes maximum.

- Get attention: Capture the viewer's attention in the first 10 seconds with relevant information.

- Show them what you do: Break up the video with interesting graphics and other content.

- Tell a story: Customer experiences and success stories are a great way to build business.

- Have past customers create a video review of your business and you.

- Call to action: Frame your offer in terms of "problem—solution—take action". Be sure to provide an effective call to action.

- Mobile technology: Make sure your video can be seen on all devices including mobile phones, tablets and PCs.

Creating videos is one challenge for corporate marketers and communicators. Delivering them to audiences scattered around the world and using a myriad of communication devices is another. If yours is like most B2B businesses, you'll want the new video to be available in a range of file formats and able to appear on all sorts of different devices from Blackberries to iPads.

Happily, as the number of display options has increased, software vendors have been hard at work creating delivery platforms and services that make the "how" of video content delivery across different devices and in many different formats much more straightforward. Ultimately, a good delivery platform will enable you to create a single video format, seamlessly handling the conversion of this format and delivery automatically depending on the type of viewing device being used.

But wait a minute—isn't that just what YouTube does? Why shouldn't we just use YouTube as a delivery platform? It's common practice among B2B companies to post videos of various kinds to YouTube, even creating their own YouTube corporate channel. This strategy is, however, of limited efficacy, as it robs marketers of vital traffic information that can generate leads and optimize the returns on their video investments. What's really needed is YouTube-like functionality but under the ownership and control of your own company. Before you commit to a specific solution, you should consider video distribution platforms such as that of Copenhagen-based company 23. The company's 23Video service enables companies to create their own video sites, analogous to that of YouTube, and provides built-in tools to manage integration of the hosted videos with Facebook, YouTube, Twitter and more. You can track how your videos are seen, used, shared and embedded and the system supports all browsers and mobile devices including iPad, iPhone and Android.

While there is no "right" approach to successfully distributing video across the Internet, there are two vital and common-sense elements:

- The creation of compelling content that provides value to the viewer either in the form of entertainment or information (and ideally both) at one end of the process
- The appropriate and successful promotion and distribution of that content at the other

Robust analytics and clear goal setting are also very important; knowing your audience, the specific KPIs for a piece of content, and having the information to optimize that content based on the ways in which audiences are consuming and interacting with it.

Video can work effectively across all of the three Voices—it simply requires more planning ahead of implementation to deliver on its full promise.

LinkedIn

In July of 1997, Stanford graduate Reid Hoffman resigned his product management role at Fujitsu to start his own business. Called Socialnet, the new venture was meant to be a kind of online dating service that also enabled its members to find golfing partners, roommates and other like-minded people. When the business failed to get off the ground, Hoffmann was encouraged by another Stanford graduate, Peter Thiel, to join a small startup called PayPal, acting as executive vice president of product development. He accepted and became part of one of the world's online venture success stories when PayPal was sold to eBay in October 2002 for the tidy sum of US$1.5 billion.

With his pockets lined by the eBay deal, Hoffman turned his attention to the professional social networking space—something he had begun to think was particularly interesting. He established LinkedIn with his own money.

As far as Hoffman recalls, the first 13 people to join LinkedIn invited 112 others and the problem that had stopped Socialnet in its tracks—how to achieve wide distribution of an online service—seemed to be on its way to solution. In the years that followed, LinkedIn grew virally at an astounding rate. The rest, as they say, is history.

Today, LinkedIn is the market leader in serious business networking. It boasts over 150 million registered users around the globe, the majority of whom are B2B executives in a wide variety of industries. At the time of writing, LinkedIn services are available in sixteen languages—English, Czech, Dutch, French, German, Indonesian, Italian, Japanese, Korean, Malay, Portuguese, Romanian, Russian, Spanish, Swedish and Turkish—making it a truly international marketing and communications channel.

LinkedIn has rapidly become the default network for business professionals, particularly those working in B2B contexts. Unlike Facebook, YouTube or Twitter, LinkedIn has always been focused on the business world, so it's custom-designed to support commercially-oriented promotional activities. However, few B2B companies (or the executives within them) use the full potential of the network for boosting customer loyalty, generating leads or setting up partnerships and alliances.

Strategic planning for promoting your business via LinkedIn should be conducted both at an individual profile level and at company level. At the individual level, you should make sure that all appropriate employees have a personal LinkedIn profile, following guidelines for its setup and cultivation that encourage, for example, optimal use of relevant keywords, well-written resumé data and summaries, sharing of connections and regular use of Status Updates (Twitter-like informative messages broadcasted to other members of personal LinkedIn networks).

Encourage employees to feed blog posts into LinkedIn (using the available automated cross-posting tools) or provide access to slides from their recent presentations, information about upcoming speaking events and other business-oriented activities in which they're involved. Make sure your company's staff update their profiles with current information (most LinkedIn users forget or can't be bothered doing this). Outdated information may cause your business to miss out on valuable networking opportunities.

A company-level LinkedIn strategy is generally based around "LinkedIn Groups". These groups usually comprise customers, employees, investors and the like who have a genuine, interested relationship with your company. In most cases, you should set up your company's own group and look around for relevant groups to join by using industry keywords in your search. Check to see if your customers and business partners (and your competitors!) are active in the groups you're considering joining.

So what should you do with your LinkedIn group once it's set up and the members are pouring in? Work with the group in the same way as you might with your blog, Facebook or Twitter activities. Manage the community and engage with it frequently, feeding it a continual flow of valuable content. The more such activity you generate, the better the investment returns. Be warned, however. There are many poor LinkedIn groups that have been set up by enthusiastic employees then left unattended.

If you have created and nourished a responsive group, LinkedIn can also be a useful place to carry out market research, whether in the form of direct questions for your LinkedIn group or releasing an early draft of a report or paper to the group to elicit detailed feedback. Imagine, for example, posing a question on the usefulness or perhaps the pricing of a proposed new service, linking people to a page that exposes them to the service and asks for their feedback. Such queries can be effective if your group is accustomed to interaction through your LinkedIn pages.

We recommend that you connect other elements within your content network to LinkedIn, too. For example, if you're running a personal or company blog, there are a number of specialized tools you can deploy to sync your posts to your LinkedIn group. For example, the popular WordPress blogging platform offers a tool called WordPress LinkedIn Application for this purpose. You can also sync Twitter accounts, presentations from SlideShare or white papers and similar via a storage and sharing service such as Box.net.

Here are a few more tips for achieving success with your LinkedIn efforts:

- Make the most of LinkedIn's Question and Answer system—asking your own questions and answering those posed by others in the group. Submit links to articles, white papers and other thought leadership content. Use RSS feeds to automatically submit company press releases to the group.

- All employees should probably be part of your LinkedIn group too, so you'll need to create an internal campaign to get people to sign up.

- Ask your LinkedIn group members to write recommendations for your company and for specific products or services they have used. These recommendations will appear in your company profile.

- Ensure you optimize your company profile (and your own) for relevant keywords, helping to drive potential customers to your group.

- Promote your LinkedIn group wherever you can—on your website and company blogs, in email signatures, even on your business card.

As with any such online activity, ensure that your IT department has administrator access and security policies in place so that you aren't left without control if the employee who set up and administered your LinkedIn group leaves your company.

There are always a few people in every LinkedIn network who actively promote themselves, some with mindless Tweet-like messages that leave you wondering whether they have nothing to do, others with valuable opinions or news. What all such efforts do achieve, however, is that they put their authors top-of-mind, a key objective of almost any communication strategy. When you're finally in buying mode, which supplier do you think of contacting first?

Facebook

Facebook is enormous. At the time of writing, the social giant has over 850 million users, more than 50 percent of whom log on to the site every day. But, while Facebook is a must-have for consumer brands, just how relevant is it for B2B businesses?

As with LinkedIn, Facebook can be used as an earned-media Voice of Industry platform—and many companies are doing exactly that via their Facebook pages. However, using someone else's platform to support your Voice of Industry strategy robs you of precious data and control. Your brand becomes subject to any negative publicity received by Facebook (let's face it, they attract a lot of flak for changes made without consultation to their privacy policies, for example), and your ability to design the look and feel of the site (even with the Timeline functionality) as well as the user experience is limited. Perhaps most disconcerting of all is the potential Facebook has to directly market to your audiences without consulting you at all.

For companies that have realized these difficulties and who prefer to create their own Voice of Industry activities on a company-controlled site, does it make sense to incorporate Facebook in communication strategies? And how should it be done?

Here's what we recommend:

- If it suits your offerings, audiences and resources, build a presence on Facebook in the form of a Facebook page, leveraging content created for your own Voice of Industry platform.

- Use Facebook to show off the people and personalities that make up your organization.

- Use Facebook's Social Plugins to socially accelerate the spread of your website content.

Let's examine those three recommendations in more detail.

(a) Leverage your content

Begin by building an active company page on Facebook. That's different from just building a static page where very little or nothing is happening. How can you make your page active? Start encouraging people to Like your page. Be sure to post interesting content from the other parts of your Three Voices™ strategy. And of course, monitor what's going on and get involved in the conversations.

Your Facebook page will benefit from an attractive visual design—and plenty of images or videos to make it more pleasing to the senses. There are no limits to what you can show (at least, not in terms of its commercial nature, provided that your content complies with Facebook's guidelines) so go ahead with anything that supports both formal and more approachable forms of communication. Showcase your products and include product information as well as links to more details.

The more customer engagement you can encourage, the better. So, for example, invite your customers to send in images of your products in use and to tell you about their experiences. If your company is a service provider, show images of your teams at work, preferably together with customers—after all, that's what Facebook is about: people and the connections between them. Highlight all the things you are doing in offline contexts, too—show images of the latest company T-shirt (and where customers might get theirs) as well as events organized by the company or ones you plan to attend.

Remember, of course, to think about calls to action. As often as possible, and within the bounds of decency, tell visitors to your Facebook page what their next move could be. For example, "Download the white paper" or "Request a free trial".

Facebook as testimonial generator
When e-commerce shopping cart software provider BigCommerce asked its B2B Facebook fan base whether any of them had seen a boost in sales from the company's recently launched Facebook shopping application, 15 companies identified themselves within 24 hours and were willing to talk to the media about their success.

(b) Make it personal
On his webbiquity blog, Tom Pick suggests that Facebook is ideal for showcasing the personal side of your organization and your employees:

Because of the intimate, informal nature of Facebook, it is the ideal venue to showcase personal content related to your company that may not be appropriate on a corporate website or even a LinkedIn profile. Many employees within B2B companies have email communication with customers and prospects, but never actually talk to them. Or they have phone conversations but never meet face to face. Facebook provides an excellent means for sharing photos and even (limited) personal information, to help put a human face on an organization, and "put a face with the name" or voice of an employee for customers and prospects.

Just a few examples of content that work better on Facebook than in more formal settings are:

- Photos of employees in casual office settings
- Photos of employees and customers interacting, or casual shots of a customer using a product (with permission, of course)
- Trade show photos
- Pictures of employees working on community service projects
- Company executives speaking, accepting awards, meeting with VIPs, etc.

- Photos of production facilities (for manufactured products)

- Photos taken with resellers or channel partners

- Informal or even humorous videos, such as HubSpot's spoof of The Office or Resco's "border battle" video shot before last season's first Vikings-Packers game

- And of course, interaction! Most customers and prospects probably won't want to interact with your brand on Facebook, but for those who do, it's important to engage them through this channel

In short, Facebook provides a place to show the human side of your company, to cut loose just a bit and have some fun. While it may produce a lead now and then, it isn't a very effective lead generation vehicle. Instead, by humanizing your company and giving a glimpse inside, its business value lies primarily in lead nurturing—helping move leads through the buying process. It's more about making current sales cycles more productive than about generating potential new business.

(c) Use social plugins

Some of the most effective Facebook features don't even happen on Facebook: Facebook's Social Plugins (the most important of which from our perspective include the Like and Send buttons, Activity Feed and Registration) enable any website to become part of the Facebook experience and, with appropriate thought, can socially supercharge your website.

Including social plugin tags on your web page makes your page equivalent to a Facebook page. This means that when a user clicks a Like button on your page, a connection is made between your page and the user. Your page will appear in the "Likes and Interests" section of the user's profile, and you have the ability to publish updates to the user.

Opinions are divided as to whether Facebook is a useful lead generator for B2B businesses. For most B2B businesses, our suggestion is to stay focused on owned media for your core traffic destinations—using Facebook further down the track once you have firmly established your Three Voices™ capabilities.

Google+

As we prepare this book for publication, the future of Google+ remains to be seen. However its growth since its launch in June 2011 is best described as meteoric – it's the fastest growing social network ever.

Here's what we know so far:

- Three weeks into the invite-only release of Google+, Google CEO Larry Page announced that the new service already had more than 10 million users, with over 1 billion items shared and received in a single day.

- By the end of 2011, Google+ had signed up 90 million users.

- At least 60% of those users log in daily.

- At least 80% of them log in weekly.

- In November 2011 Google introduced Google+ Pages for Business. Marketers were quick to sign up: by the end of 2011 there were more than 1 million business pages on Google+.

In January 2012, Google integrated Google+ into its Search results. Now, those logged in to any Google account (including Google+, iGoogle or Gmail) can choose whether to see search results that are shaped by their own personal networks. Those who choose personally flavored results will be shown recommendations from their networks that typically include links to Google+ Business Pages. Inevitably, marketers have been scrambling to develop a presence on Google+ to help with their search optimization strategies.

Our recommendation: You need a Google+ Business Page to aid your presence on Google Search if nothing else. But also be proactive as Google+ grows—look for business networking opportunities through that avenue. In due course, you might find it a useful addition to your B2B repertoire.

Twitter

Should you be on Twitter? Although the site had 500 million users by February 2012, analysts suggest that only around 21 percent are active users.

"However," as social media commentator Justin Flitter noted, "take one look at who is using Twitter and you'll find a vocal, active community of industry leaders, media, public relations, marketers, parents, entrepreneurs, all influences and early adopters who are social on and offline, creating quite a buzz."

And that really is the point. Those most active on the social networks are Malcolm Gladwell's Connectors, the people who "link us up with the world... people with a special gift for bringing the world together."

Here's more food for thought: Cisco's CTO Padmasree Warrior has more than a million personal followers—which must surely bring value to her company. Several financial services companies, or others with frequent, short news updates that need to be quickly announced, have Twitter followers numbering in the hundreds of thousands. And online marketing education companies such as Markedu make the most of the service, enabling the company to communicate new courses and schedules as well as test new ideas with its growing base of course participants.

Our recommendation: use Twitter to find and follow influencers within your sector (there are plenty of automated tools to help you identify and then follow such people). However, don't spend too much time generating tweets (unless and until you qualify as an influencer yourself). Otherwise you'll mostly be talking to an audience of one.

Flickr

It's often said that a picture is worth a thousand words. In fact, scientists lead us to believe that many people are more receptive to learning through visual inputs, just as others prefer verbal-based forms of learning and still others (known as tactile or kinesthetic learners) may learn best through moving, doing and touching.

In the business world, images of all kinds are a powerful asset in search engine optimization and social media marketing, thanks to their ability (if properly tagged) to bring in traffic from image-based searches and the fact that using an image with your content is likely to improve its general attractiveness.

The power of images to attract, explain and persuade may be the reason why Flickr, a site dedicated to the storage, display and sharing of images, has become so popular in recent times. But first, let's talk about what Flickr is— and what it enables you to do. Instead of thinking of this web-based service as a Picasa-like place to store and share photos, it's probably most useful to think of Flickr as a platform for connecting with your audiences and bringing them value in a visual manner.

Flickr lets you upload, search for and share images from almost any device, label those images with rich information (such as tags, locations or people), and share them through Facebook, Twitter, email, blogs and more. The site's numbers are impressive, to say the least. At the time of writing, it housed over 6 billion images. More than 50 million professional and amateur photographers are registered users of Flickr, and there are literally millions of active groups on the site.

Flickr enables you to create what it calls "sets" and "galleries" to group images by type or use. You can create different permission levels for specific images or groups of images, enabling the general public or, for example, just your employees to access them. You can determine which images can be downloaded and by whom, who can share them, whether images can be added to a gallery and who is allowed to blog your images. You can find out which of your pictures are most popular, how searchers found you, and where they come from.

Here's where it gets interesting: Flickr users can join groups of "Like-minded people" who are interested in specific types of images (such as infographics), and who provide, share and link to similar images, using Flickr as a vibrant social network. And it's this aspect of sharing that makes Flickr a powerful search marketing tool. Adding further power to the service, images can be shared across blogs (using embedded code), Facebook, Google Gadgets and Maps, Twitter and various other online communities that have incorporated integration with Flickr.

But is Flickr valuable for B2B businesses? When the world's largest shipping group, *A.P. Moller Maersk*, deployed a dedicated site (www.worldslargestship.com) to promote the purchase of ten more new Triple-E ships, the company used Flickr as part of its promotional strategy, placing illustrations and photographs of the impressive, energy-efficient ships on the Flickr site. Visitors to the company's Flickr channel are able to browse the various images, share them with others in their social network and comment on each image.

So while it certainly isn't the first thing that comes to most people's minds when thinking about B2B marketing and communication, the service has unique capabilities that can be a useful part of your promotional strategy.

Perhaps Flickr's most valuable contribution to B2B businesses lies in the fact that many B2B companies have complex stories to tell. Flickr is useful as yet another way to split up and structure the storytelling task. Alongside video, the service can also bring corporate messages to life for people who are primarily driven by visual communication forms rather than verbal.

But Flickr shouldn't be seen as a primarily commercial platform. Overly self-promoting sites can be—and often are—removed by Flickr employees, which could mean the waste of your company's resources, including many man hours. In the words of industry commentator Richard Burkhardt, "Flickr just wants Polaroid moments". Flickr itself prefers to say that it expects people to use their accounts "…to share photos, not to sell things."

Using your Flickr account to host graphic elements of web page designs, logos, icons, and other non-photographic elements is prohibited, as is directly selling products or services via the site. The site's terms of use also frown upon using an account solely as a product catalog or linking to commercial sites from the collections of photos attached to each account, which it calls "photostreams".

To stay on the safe side, you should (in Flickr's own words) "seek to upload fresh, authentic material rather than product shots or staged, over-produced content that would be more at home in your product catalog or latest advertising campaign".

Don't let that discourage you, however, from deploying Flickr in your communication strategy. Flickr is entirely open to the following examples of content, as recommended on the company's website:

- A bike shop owner shares photos of happy customers in his store.
- A clothes manufacturer shares behind-the-scenes action from its factory.
- A tech company shares a video of its community volunteer event.
- A government space organization shares photos of recent satellite captures.
- An NGO shares photos of disaster relief efforts.

In other words, Flickr likes to see engaging content. Deliver on that promise and you should have no problems. In any case, before linking to any sales-focused information, you should check out Flickr's latest terms of service to make sure that you aren't in violation as these terms are subject to change from time to time.

Bearing the above comments in mind, what kind of images should you consider placing on Flickr? Here's a list of what we consider to be suitable options for B2B companies:

- Pictures that tell stories

- Products presented in interesting ways rather than catalog-like shots

- Diagrams and infographics (include links to find out more)

- Executive headshots (include bios in the caption boxes).

- Company history (the napkin that started the whole thing off?)

- Imagery from white papers and other reports
  (include links to them plus commentary)

- Corporate map of locations ("we're global")

- Movie-style posters that promote your podcasts, videos,
  LinkedIn groups and more

- Buildings and facilities (include text about what a great place
  it is to work!)

- Presentations (key imagery and, potentially, entire presentations
  within Flickr usage guidelines)

- Trade show pictures—candid shots of your visitors, staff,
  memorable moments

- Awards (put excerpts from your award application in caption boxes)

- Employees enjoying their work or social events that show off
  your culture

- Customers interacting with your company

Don't rush to put all your images up on Flickr. Instead, think carefully whether the images you're uploading will really engage your company's audiences. Are they of sufficient quality from a visual standpoint (e.g. sufficiently high resolution)? Would you be happy for them to be picked up and used by a journalist? Don't lock your images up under copyright, but place as many as possible under a Creative Commons license to enable the widest possible distribution and use by viewers.

You can also create special areas on the Flickr site to tell specific stories about your organization or your projects. For example, you may want to encourage current and former employees or other stakeholders to contribute photos that tell the story of your company's creation and development over the years—or that of a particularly successful product or project. Make sure, of course, to ask contributors to include whatever (non-sensitive) information they can with each image.

As an element of your Voice of Industry strategy, you can also start up image-oriented communities on Flickr focused around specific industry challenges or opportunities, or simply celebrate the intrinsic appeal of your industry. Use RSS feeds to keep in touch with community members. Incorporate Flickr's traffic statistics for each image into your metrics and learn from them so that you can fine-tune your image-based content.

You will also want to investigate what other industry interest groups may already exist on Flickr and join those you feel are appropriate, even if it's just to keep in touch with what's going on in the group (for example, how are your competitors using the service, what can you learn from this?).

And of course, in your corporate social media guidelines do remember to include both encouragement to use Flickr and guidelines for its use by employees. Explain how to tag your images and which types of images should be assigned various levels of permission.

Think "content assets" and increase your ROI

Here's how to get more out of each article, video or photographic image you produce: think about each item as a content asset. By this we mean a reusable, re-packageable, updateable element that can be used in multiple contexts.

Let's consider an example. Imagine you have a customer who has agreed to let your company write a case study about his business. Ideally, you should think about how many different content assets you can generate from this interaction. Can you have a writer and photographer visit the client? Can you take a variety of photos of the person being interviewed? Can the photographer use a hand-held video camera and a lapel microphone to capture the person repeating several of the points he or she makes in, say, one-minute takes? Or even record the entire interview with a single camera focused on the interviewee as he/she talks to your writer? While you've got your team there, can you get shots of the customer's products, building, or a corporate logo in the reception area?

Of course, you may not yet know in which ways you might use all of these items, but having content assets like these on hand are a quick way to come up with inexpensive, easily spreadable ideas. Now imagine your writer is interviewing the client. Can he record the interview? Careful planning before the meeting could enable the writer to ask the client a standard set of questions that fit neatly into a podcast "show" that's part of a series of case study podcasts. The same set of questions (or rather, the answers to those questions) can then be turned into several written pieces of content: a case study article of the usual kind, a question/answer-based interview article that boosts perceived authenticity for the reader, customer quotes that can be tweeted—the list is endless.

What about the video footage your photographer has just captured? As long as the sound quality and lighting turn out to be acceptable (a certain amount of "home-made" look and feel can add credibility to your videos but it's best not to overdo it), you can easily edit the footage to create a valuable library of short clips that can be used as content for your website, sales presentations, online corporate magazine, company video channel and more.

Your content strategy (and the willingness of the customer—don't forget to get the interviewee to sign an appropriate release form) will define what's possible and desirable. You can find excellent advice on the subject of interview releases on Stanford University's site at http://fairuse.stanford.edu/Copyright_and_Fair_Use_Overview/chapter12/12-d.html

Turning our attention to maximizing ROI (which we will in the next chapter), how exactly are B2B marketers measuring the success of their content-driven efforts? Data from the 2011 B2B Technology Marketing Community survey sheds some light on current practices, but it is obvious that some of the most relevant measures such as searchability and impact are missing. Their omission is most likely a sign that the majority of marketers and communicators don't have the know-how or processes in place to work with these types of metrics.

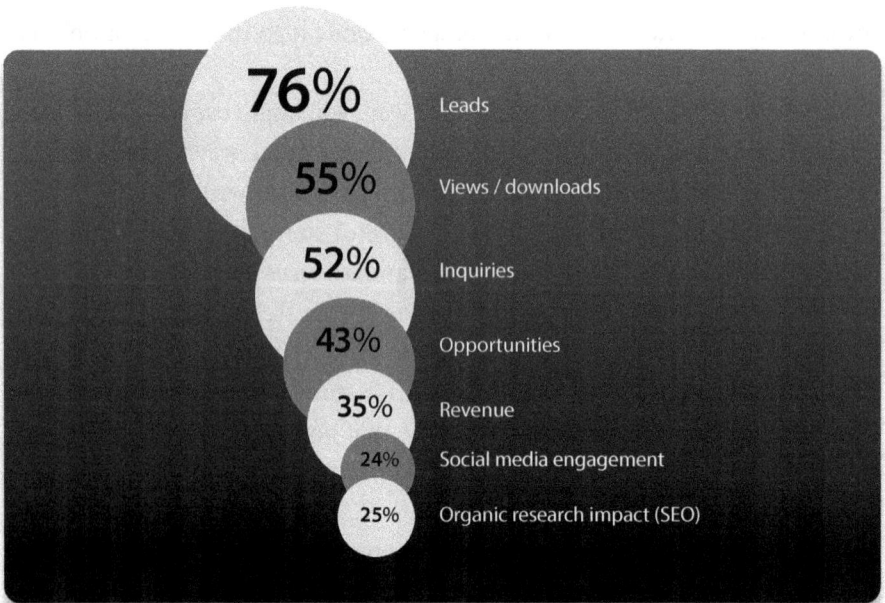

76%	Leads
55%	Views / downloads
52%	Inquiries
43%	Opportunities
35%	Revenue
24%	Social media engagement
25%	Organic research impact (SEO)

Source: B2B Technology Marketing Community 2011 survey

Figure 6.1 How do marketers measure content marketing success?

Key take-outs

- There is a wide range of media that can support your Voice of Company, Voice of Industry and Voice of Customer activities.

- Blogs can display a vibrant corporate culture—a more human side of the company and a way for stakeholders to build trust and engagement but ideally should be created by one highly motivated person.

- Properly executed business podcasts can build a recurring audience if there is a carefully tailored concept with a clear editorial mission, and attention to production values such as sound quality and the presenter's style.

- Webinars are seminars transmitted over the Internet by one or more presenters or panellists to a large audience at a particular time, particularly relevant in B2B contexts where products are often technically complex and difficult to describe in a simple product brochure.

- The success of B2B webinars is directly linked to the level of interactivity provided during the session as well as careful planning, engagement and follow-up after the event.

- Informative, entertaining videos are more engaging, more interactive and more personal than most other forms of content—and they drive search results like no other medium.

- The B2B market is ready for video but B2B marketing and communication budgets are not, and companies have only just begun to think about how to maximize video investments via the Internet.

- LinkedIn is a necessary part of most B2B strategies, although access to user data as well as customization capabilities are limited.

- Facebook may be used as a Voice of Customer platform but the user experience is limited and so is your control of what happens on the site.

- The still-growing Google+ is now an important factor to consider in search optimization.

- Twitter is useful for finding and following influencers within your sector; its use as a B2B promotional tool can vary.

- B2B companies with complex stories to tell can use Flickr to split up and structure the storytelling task via visual communication such as infographics.

Notes

CHAPTER SEVEN

The business case for
a Three Voices™ strategy

Does a Three Voices™ strategy lead to increased sales?

The most challenging activities of B2B marketers tend to center around generating high-quality leads and getting their messages to a larger section of their potential audience. In fact, a 2012 report from BtoB Online and Bizo, drawing upon a survey of 326 US-based B2B marketers, saw some 61 percent of respondents say that generating more leads and reaching more of their audience are their biggest marketing challenges for the year. Respondents also mentioned the need to market to a growing number of people in the buying process and support ever-lengthening sales cycles.

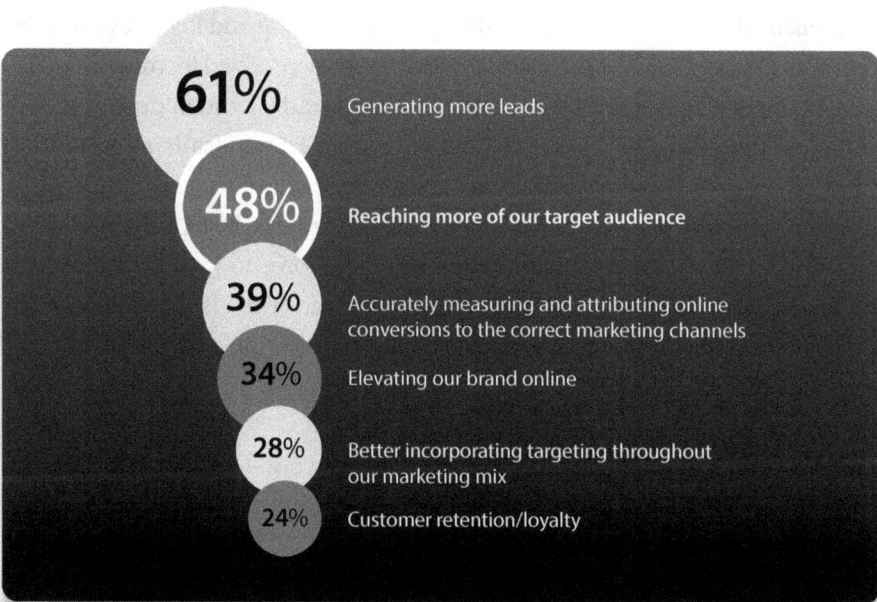

61% Generating more leads

48% Reaching more of our target audience

39% Accurately measuring and attributing online conversions to the correct marketing channels

34% Elevating our brand online

28% Better incorporating targeting throughout our marketing mix

24% Customer retention/loyalty

Source: BtoB Magazine: Online Marketing: The Next Frontier, March 2012

Figure 7.1 Today's most significant B2B marketing challenges.

Can a market approach based on Three Voices™ strategy help to achieve these aims? Can it actually result in increased sales? That's the million-dollar (or more) question we're often asked. And it's not always easy to answer. One problem is that most B2B companies don't sell their wares via some slick e-commerce site that enables clear, traceable measurement of incentives and conversion processes. Instead, the nature of a typical B2B transaction often dictates long and complex sales cycles where it's hard to attribute the final sale to any particular milestone along the way.

It's hard to deny, however, that greater levels of engagement, trust and information dissemination between the company and its stakeholders are likely to create a better platform for commercial success. Content marketing, as a specific discipline, has plenty of evidence demonstrating increases in attention to companies, including strong advances in the number of leads, for example. Mike Volpe, CMO of HubSpot, provides the example of a 300-person division of a 5,000-employee global industrial company that designs and manufactures systems for climate, smoke and ventilation control systems. The company increased its web traffic by 1,000 percent by starting a blog, optimizing for SEO, and leveraging social media.

Mike also tells of Lynden, Inc., a 2,000-person shipping and logistics company that was able to grow the number of quote requests received by more than 270 percent, bringing the sales team more qualified leads. Lynden deployed both in-bound marketing and Voice of Company optimization (calls-to-action and multiple targeted landing pages) to achieve its result. It's a great illustration of where much of the value of a Three Voices™ strategy lies: in the growth of qualified leads available for your company's sales force to work with. If you're on the right track with your strategy, then those leads will also be feeling pretty positive toward your company and its offerings, creating a better entry point for salespeople.

One way to begin analyzing the likely benefits of your Three Voices™ strategy is by considering a key activity for many B2B businesses: the product launch.

Boosting B2B product launches via market buzz

Many B2B companies focus their activities on that most holy of events, the product launch. The entire company tends to run like mad toward each launch just as small boys playing football all swarm around the ball, leaving the remainder of the playing field practically empty. It's a costly affair, and one upon which the company's sales and organizational energy can be highly dependent. But this kind of traditional, explosive product launch is quickly becoming a dinosaur.

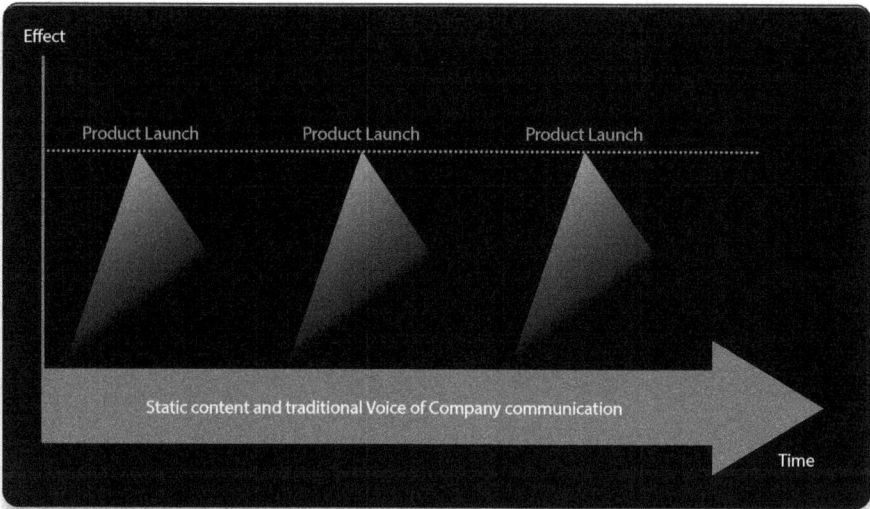

Figure 7.2 Even today, most B2B companies treat each new product introduction as a separate, high-cost activity.

Instead of these sporadic, all-or-nothing investments, smart marketers are looking at the big picture and investing in ways to create and exploit market buzz (and increase the number of people connected to the company) on an ongoing basis. By "buzz" we mean things like:

Pre-launch
- Heightening market awareness and priorization of the pain points your product will address
- Carefully staged leaks that your company is working on a revolutionary new product

- Rumors about a pending product release to address the pain points

- Beta program participation and discussion

- Previews to key influencers

- Opt-in list building

- Product readiness validation

Launch
- Traffic ramp-up

- Sales ramp-up

- Scarcity motivation

- Social proof from influencers

Post-launch
- Proliferation of product success stories

- Influencer endorsement

- Rapid market feedback

Many of the above elements are new to the product launch processes of most B2B companies. While various makeshift programs with similar aims have been attempted in the past, they have been difficult to manage and have added little real power to product introductions.

Now, however, with the arrival of the new breed of B2B buyer—one who is far more online-oriented and gathers a larger proportion of his or her decision-support information from sources other than the manufacturer—things have definitely changed. Today, by leveraging existing online B2B buyer forums—or better still, by owning and operating online Voice of Industry platforms where your prospects and customers can conduct their discussions—there is a great opportunity both to magnify the impact of product launches and reduce the cost per launch.

Take the extreme case of Apple, for example. There are so many conversations going on about the company and its products, many of them in Apple-specific forums (both official and unofficial), that all it takes is for a senior company executive to write one sentence in a blog announcing an upcoming press conference and the message will spread like wildfire, with customers speculating on possible product enhancements and desperately eager to find out more. Could Dell do the same? Or any of Apple's other competitors?

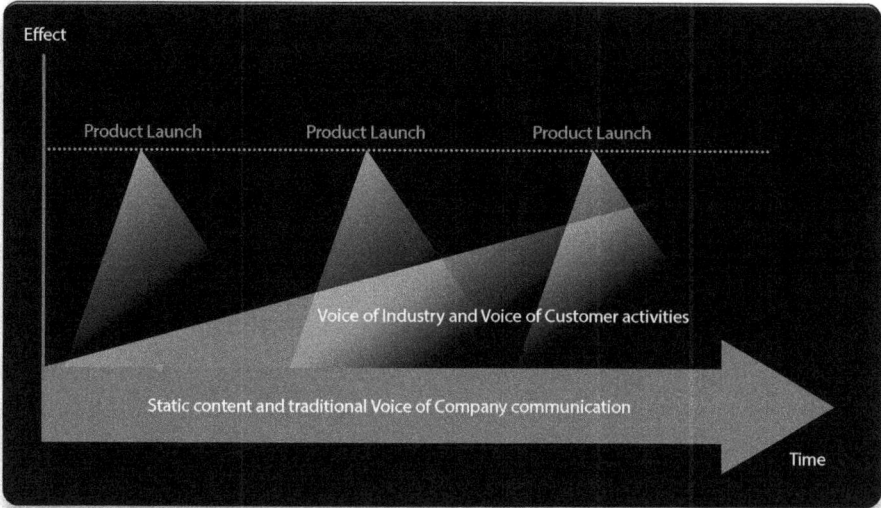

Figure 7.3 Companies that have built up a significant online presence require far fewer resources to achieve the same impact when releasing new products.

Of course, Apple's market buzz machine has been built up over many years and is also the result of an impressive legacy of product innovation. But B2B companies of lesser fame can still achieve significant gains by actively building their own online Voice of Industry sites and adding fuel to the conversations among their prospects and customers.

What if your company were to do something similar—or put more effort into the buzz generation activities you may already be doing? What effect might it have to set up one or more industry-specific communities complete with regular newsletters? Of course, there are initial planning and setup costs that, for most companies, will be significantly larger than the resources required for a single product launch. Thereafter, however, ongoing operating costs should be relatively contained.

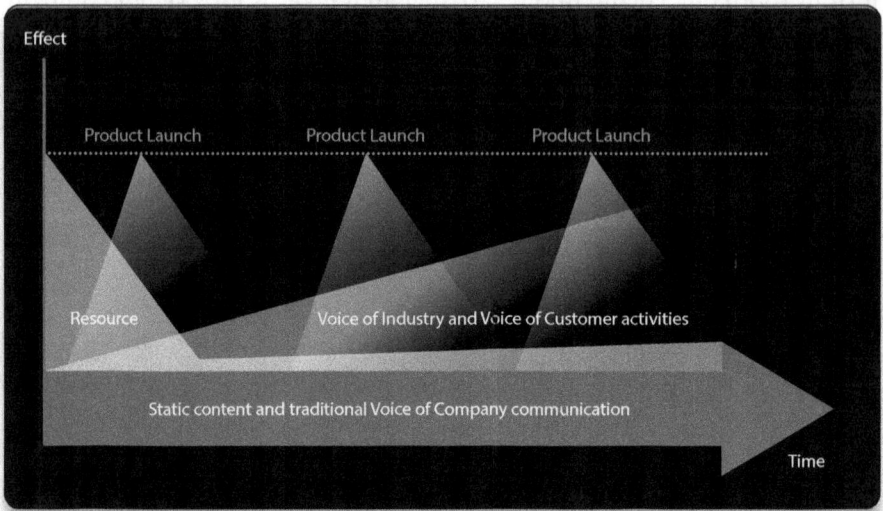

Figure 7.4 After initial setup costs, the operating costs of working with online industry communities are relatively contained.

Over time, as the numbers of prospects, customers and other industry players flourish in your Three Voices™ "ecosystem", you will start to see returns on your investment that quickly surpass the initial costs of the project. And you are likely to discover that your close contact with potential buyers results not only in better product launches, but also in more customer-focused product development and faster access to and incorporation of vital market feedback.

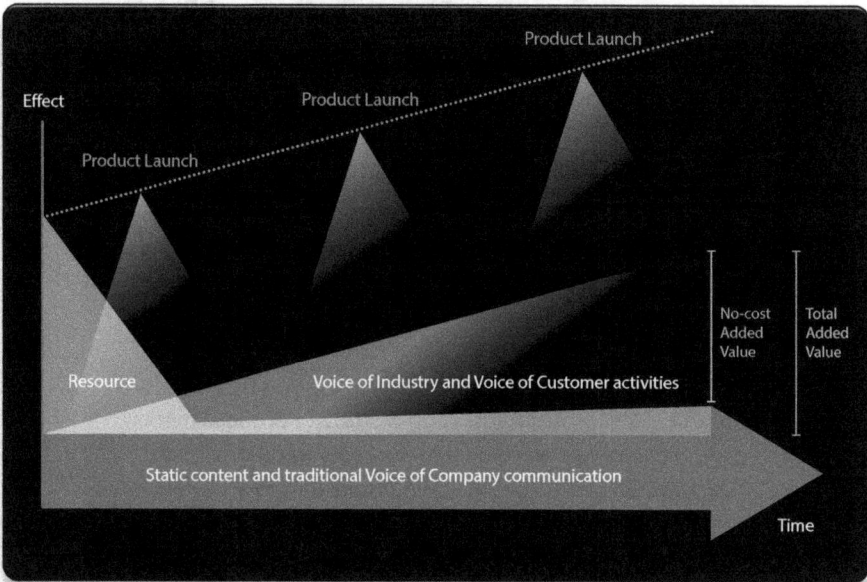

Figure 7.5 As your Three Voices™ activities grow, a no-cost component begins to appear, enabling your company to extract greater ROI from its investments.

Working this way is not a matter of whether to change your marketing approach to product launches and many other marketing activities, but when to do it. And that allows you to choose whether to be the first in your industry to move or to make your move later, hoping to benefit from the first mover's mistakes. Just remember, of course, that thought leadership does point toward being the one that leads the pack.

CASE STUDY

CISCO EMBRACES THE NEW AGE OF PRODUCT LAUNCHES

What might happen if a B2B company decided to launch an important new, highly priced item via social media alone? That's what Cisco decided to investigate with the launch of its Aggregation Services Router, a product costing over a million dollars. The result—generated as far back as 2008—became one of the top six product launches in the history of the company, and a major factor in gaining internal support for this type of "powered-up" launch.

Before this initial attempt at harnessing the power of social media, Cisco's product launches followed a predictably traditional path. The CEO or another senior executive would present to an audience of Cisco staff, press and outside influencers flown in from around the world. Press releases would be distributed, customers emailed about the new product, print ads created and distributed.

The new, social media-focused launch was conducted purely online, even including a Second Life launch event with chairs and palm trees for the audience. Given the enthusiastic gaming habits of networking engineers, Cisco also created a game to help their audience learn about the product while playing.

Assisted by YouTube, videoconferencing, mobile and Facebook activities, the extra boost to Cisco's product launch was astounding. Overall, the launch incurred just one-sixth the cost of a typical product launch. Yet the launch event reached 90 times more people than in the past, three times as much press coverage was generated, and over 1,000 blog posts and 40 million online impressions were created. At the same time, the company estimated a saving of around 42,000 gallons of gas!

In comments made to Social Media Examiner, LaSandra Brill, Cisco's senior manager of global social media, was reported as saying: "Social media doesn't replace the need for white papers or sales interaction. I think it helps accelerate and shorten the sales cycle. There are studies out there that people who are involved in communities and engaged with the brand are likely to spend up to 50 percent more than those who are not. We want to try to prove that."

Benefits beyond marketing and communications

So far, we've focused mostly on how your marketing and communication efforts can be enhanced by implementing a stakeholder engagement platform that enables you to leverage the three Voices. But there are new and improved capabilities for other parts of the organization, too—all of which can strengthen the business case for applying resources in this direction.

The benefits of improved customer understanding

Imagine you've implemented your Three Voices™ strategy. Now, as the owner and operator of one or more Voice of Industry platforms, you get unprecedented access not just to what customers are saying about their habits and preferences in discussion sections, but also to how they actually behave.

Market-related decisions facing your company will now be informed by extensive, validated data on, for example, how registered leads interact with the site, where visitors abandon the website, time spent on specific pages, where visitors enter your website, the percentage of visitors who take action (register, download a content item, etc.), and so on. Statistics like these can help you to identify which content is actually of most interest to your audiences. And they add valuable data to the inputs and conversations experienced on your Voice of Industry sites, via Voice of Customer communities and participation in other external forums.

Based on these activities and the rest of your Three Voices™ efforts, you'll be able to track not just who knows about you but also who truly engages with you, and where your influence spreads elsewhere across both online and offline worlds. You will also gain valuable insights into barriers to conversion, possible issues with your products, and the potential for entry into new markets, among other things.

The upsides for innovation

In decades of working with innovation and product development, we've watched and participated in the efforts of many B2B companies to come up with ideas, evaluate and choose potential winners, then attempt to take the resulting shortlist through the stages toward product launch.

It's one of those situations where the old saying "It's better to do the right thing than to do things right" truly applies. A powerful idea that solves relevant and pressing market pains or enables significant new capabilities will most likely endure and become a profitable venture. That's why ideation (the process of coming up with new ideas) is the lifeblood of innovation. But coming up with the *right* informed insights and fresh ideas is what really matters—and that requires getting much more in touch with market conversations than most B2B companies are today.

Here's our conviction: Your Voice of Industry and Voice of Customer activities have the potential to revolutionize the way your company performs its ideation, evaluation and development processes in several ways:

- Up-to-date market intelligence
- The ability to enter into dialogue with prospects and customers
- Guidance from those who will actually have to use your new products
- A constant flow of fresh energy and ideas
- A ready and willing test bed for product trials
- More and better feedback

The upsides for HR

For most companies, particularly those involved in knowledge-heavy industries, recruiting and retaining highly skilled workers is of vital strategic importance. Talented people are hard to find—and retaining them is becoming even tougher. In some sectors, such as wind energy, management consulting and IT, the competition for talent is particularly intense. A properly executed content network comprising the three Voices can add both reach and power to recruiting efforts.

Reach

Before you can make it onto a job-seeker's shortlist, they need to be made aware that you exist. While that's usually not a problem for well-known brands, lesser-known B2B companies generally do a poor job of employer branding and may only be known to people who already work within the industry, perhaps only in a single geographic region.

A well-implemented stakeholder engagement platform that leverages the three Voices has at its core a great deal of content that is enjoyed, linked to and shared, thus achieving higher visibility in search results. At the same time, the new alliances and partnerships that such an approach encourages are likely to open doors to new flows of applicants. Ensuring that you address and involve educational institutions, too, should be a part of any forward-looking engagement platform, and will give you easier access to graduating talent.

CASE STUDY

RECRUITING TALENT

Using Three Voices™ strategy to lure talented employees, Michael Frahm, director of a small talent recruiting agency, focused on bringing the cream of India's university graduates to work for some of Scandinavia's top-performing companies. According to Frahm, on Jobs Day, when the graduates are ready to leave their institutions, their short lists of desired workplaces are dominated by the household names—Google, Microsoft, Apple and other Fortune 500 companies. They flock to the booths of such companies who can then select the best of the best ahead of lesser known businesses. Frahm emphasizes the importance of encouraging early connections with promising students in order to secure a place on their employer short lists after graduation. Voice of Industry sites and Voice of Customer listening and responding efforts, he says, are an excellent way to build such connections, because they enable companies to build their reputations as thought leaders in an appealing, credible manner well ahead of graduation.

Power

Highly skilled workers are often keen to work with the thought leaders in their industry—those companies that are perceived to be the most innovative in the way they think and in the solutions they offer their customers. As a company that makes its thought leadership apparent via a Three Voices™ strategy, you should expect your company's image as an exciting employer to be boosted beyond many of your competitors. Perception is, as they say, reality!

Social media has been convincingly shown not only to aid recruitment but to increase employee retention, too. If your Three Voices™ strategy enables employees to profile their knowledge, expand their skills and network, and generally become enriched, you are likely to also be improving their working environment and their long-term career opportunities. You may also find it beneficial to elevate specific employees to "star status" within your Three Voices™ ecosystem, firmly connecting their position and status in the industry with your company's brand (à la Sony's Jim Scott).

Another reason to connect the organization's thinking about employee retention to your new Three Voices™ strategy is the opportunity for individuals to use their creativity—something which has long been known to improve job satisfaction. Facilitating creativity via the three Voices may involve, for example, setting up online idea forums or introducing topics for organization- or department-wide discussion. Above all, make sure your company doesn't stifle such creativity by restricting access to social media such as Facebook—a corporate malpractice that has unfortunately become far too commonplace in an attempt to deal with an entirely different issue, that of general employee motivation.

CASE STUDY

CREATIVE ACCOUNTING

In 2007, the global consulting and accountancy giant Deloitte kicked off its Deloitte Film Festival event as a human resources initiative. Employees were asked to create short videos in response to the question, "What's your Deloitte?" They were allowed to work in teams of one to seven people to make videos reflecting their experiences of working for the company. Over 370 submissions were received with 2,000 people taking part in the making of the films. Videos were posted on a special YouTube-like area on the intranet and then rated by colleagues. Overall, more than half of the staff engaged with the initiative. The channel has had over 400,000 views, and 33 percent of staff reported they felt greater loyalty to the company as a result. The top videos, which now appear on YouTube, became part of Deloitte's on-going recruitment efforts.

Not all human resource departments are quick to adopt new ways of working. In fact, a 2010 survey conducted by Melcrum and reported in Personnel Today found that of 2,600 respondents, only 11 percent said they had used social media to the benefit of their HR department. So don't expect HR managers to beat down your door to use the potential benefits from your Three Voices™ strategy. But do let them know about the new capabilities and find ways to incorporate their needs in the content and partnerships you create.

> "When we are recruiting, a CV shows us a candidate's education, skill-set and experience. But what you can't show on a CV (but can through social media) is personality, attitude, connections and values. Social media helps us to understand the person and how they might fit into our workplace culture."

Ben Acott *thinktank media*

...

The benefits for customer service

There's plenty of evidence that elements of a Three Voices™ strategy can reduce the costs of customer service while increasing customer satisfaction—which is far from the usual outcome of such reductions. For example, InfusionSoft, a provider of marketing automation software for small enterprises, primarily supports its customers via a community that blends Voice of Company with Voice of Customer-style discussions.

InfusionSoft's aim was to use its community of registered users to create a knowledge base and improved capabilities for its customers to ask questions of the company, search for answers to previously raised issues, engage in discussions with other customers, and even help to solve the issues raised by their peers.

Direct savings ensued, with the number of customer service agents required to support customers dropping from one agent for every 72 customers to one for every 172 customers. At the same time, customer satisfaction increased by some 10 percentage points. Given the role of customer satisfaction as a driver of repeat business and referrals, the company considered these improvements likely to amount to a significant pay-off.

In March 2011, at The Fusion Marketing Experience in Brussels, Belgium, Olivier Blanchard demonstrated how customer service can leverage social media such as Twitter to reduce costs and hopefully enhance the customer experience. The points he presented, as reported by Jim Ducharme, included:

- One CSR [customer service representative *Ed.*] can handle several customers at once.
- Customers are not stuck on hold listening to bad music or repetitive recordings telling them why their call is so important.
- "Accents" are no longer an issue.
- Resolution times remain the same but to the customer, they seem considerably shorter.
- CSRs spend less time on each ticket.
- 140 characters keeps things simple.
- Transparency of process translates to positive PR.
- Added convenience for customers on the go.
- Proactive customer service can generate loyalty and capture market share (angry customers could be a competitor's customers).
- Even a 10% shift to Twitter customer service could yield significant savings.

Olivier also called attention to the multi-channel world in which we live today and the fact that the more options you offer for customers and prospects to interact with you, the better. A Three Voices™ strategy enables a broad range of interaction possibilities, serving your customers in the contexts and on the devices they prefer.

The fictitious example of Life Rafts, Inc.

If you've read this book thus far, then you understand the need to have your B2B brand speak with three different Voices: Voice of Company, Voice of Industry and Voice of Customer, each with its communication platform, role and degree of credibility. Now you are ready to consider how to manage their interactions. Working together, the Three Voices™ can create a far greater return on your investment than if each existed in isolation.

To show you how it works, let's examine an example of a (fictitious) life raft manufacturer, Life Rafts, Inc., a Florida-based business bent on increasing its share of the booming marine safety equipment market.

The company's well-designed communication strategy has led to the creation of a platform for each of the three Voices.

On the Voice of Company side:

- The company's website communicates corporate and product messages.

- A variety of offline events and materials describe the company's products and services in a straightforward, helpful manner, ensuring a pleasant customer experience.

- Print and interactive versions of a company-centric newsletter, *RaftLife*, circulate every quarter to a growing database of subscribers.

- Life Rafts, Inc.'s brand is convincingly presented, drawing upon both rational and emotional elements with its value propositions and the way these are expressed. Boastfulness is kept to a minimum.

The company's Voice of Industry activities include:

- *Which Liferaft?*, a company-owned and operated industry news and content site with some 5,000 visitors viewing its articles and video-based blog each month.

- Contributions of content to, and sourcing of relevant content from a small group of content partners including one of the industry's largest distributors of marine equipment.

- A *Which Liferaft?* newsletter, generated monthly by aggregating and editing content from the site. It's emailed to a base of 1,500 invitation-only subscribers.

- A popular industry community called*"Afloat"*, where around 500 registered members chat online about issues related to the liferaft industry and more than 3,000 visitors read the conversation threads.

- An extended network of external industry experts and partners (non-competing, value-adding) that participate in discussions and distribute or link to *Which Liferaft?* discussions and content.

- Significant professional communities across selected external social media such as LinkedIn (3,000 members) and Twitter (8,000 followers) which serve as distribution and conversation platforms for *Which Liferaft?* content and community.

- Offline *Afloat* events in major cities with speakers from within and beyond the company.

- On-going *Afloat* webinars on the topic of marine safety, featuring a mix of internal and external subject matter experts.

- A solid SEO and SEM strategy captures prospects searching for information on life rafts and marine safety in general.

- Paid media in the form of banner ads and small print ads in trade publications—although this is being slowly phased out as momentum grows for *Which Liferaft?* and *Afloat.*

Over time, *Which Liferaft?* has grown in industry influence to the point that policy makers and market regulators partner with the platform to gain industry feedback and disseminate news and information.

Life Rafts, Inc.'s Voice of Customer activities are divided into continuous and campaign-based listening programs:

- The company uses Google Analytics and other free software tools to constantly monitor online social media conversations related to keywords and phrases such as "life raft" or "marine safety".

- Customer satisfaction surveys are conducted at regular intervals.

- Whenever a large group of customers gather—as part of a new product launch, for example—the marketing department looks for opportunities to interview them on video or capture their viewpoints in structured questionnaires that can provide fuel the creation of peer surveys (a particularly compelling type of content).

- Prior to each new product release or other form of campaign, listening activities collect data on market conversations to help guide the campaign's design.

- Following each campaign, specific listening activities measure its impact on a set of KPIs.

Here's how each of the company's functions could interact with these platforms:

- The Marketing department monitors the conversations among prospects and customers on *Afloat* to understand what demand might exist for specific new products or services.

- R&D has started a conversation topic on *Afloat* to help figure out how to solve a technical obstacle.

- The CEO's recent speech at a key industry event is featured on *Which Liferaft?*'s home page.

- The Sales Director visits *Which Liferaft?* regularly to keep up to date with what his own company and external experts are saying about industry directions.

- The sales force forwards topic-specific links to content from the interactive edition of the *Which Liferaft?* newsletter to prospects. They especially like videos of the company's subject matter experts talking about new offerings and industry issues because it just seems more credible.

- Quality Assurance notes that a material used for life raft production by competitors is being praised on *Afloat* for its durability—and forwards that information to R&D.

- Corporate Communications can see that articles about sustainability on the *Which Liferaft?* site are attracting a lot of attention—and decides to create a new article calling attention to Life Rafts, Inc.'s latest philanthropic venture in Venezuela.

- Upon seeing the attention attracted by a conversation about a current problem with life rafts that will be solved by Life Rafts, Inc.'s next product launch, Marketing decides to pre-release some information, publishing it on the company's own website then providing a link to the information during a conversation on *Afloat*.

Sound too difficult? If you're like most people to whom we describe this bright future, you're probably wondering how on earth your organization can cope with the change—and whether you can manage the effort without having to significantly rearrange your life. We understand your concerns and we'll address some of them in the next chapter, which delves into just what it takes to execute a Three Voices™ strategy for a typical B2B business.

Key take-outs

- Greater levels of engagement, trust and information dissemination between the company and its stakeholders should create a better platform for commercial success.

- When talking about a Three Voices™ strategy, we're also talking about a large part of your company's future activities (not just marketing and communications).

- Product launches can be greatly assisted by a Three Voices™ strategy—made more powerful and cost-effective by attention to what happens before, during and after the launch.

- Close contact with potential buyers may result in better product launches, more accurate product development and vital market feedback.

- A Three Voices™ strategy enhances customer understanding—you can get unprecedented access not just to what customers say about their own interests and habits, but also to how they *actually* behave.

- Voice of Industry and Voice of Customer activities have the potential to revolutionize the way your company performs its ideation, evaluation and development processes.

- A Three Voices™ strategy can add both reach and power to recruiting efforts for your HR department.

- A Three Voices™ strategy can also enhance customer service capabilities, improving service and reducing costs of service.

- Working together, the three Voices can create a far greater return on your investment than if each were operated in isolation.

Notes

CHAPTER EIGHT:

Building a Three Voices™ strategy—step by step

There are many ways to approach the planning and implementation of a Three Voices™ strategy—each of which will have its own benefits, challenges and learning curve. In this chapter, we provide an overview of how our own particular methodology is presently structured, detailing the various steps a company can take to revolutionize the way it interacts with its stakeholders. Follow this methodology religiously or just use it as input to your own.

Highly sophisticated B2B companies should be able to carry out at least some of the phases of a Three Voices™ project using internal resources. Most organizations, however, will need to bring in external expertise to assist in varying degrees across the phases. This should be seen as a learning opportunity, since the participation of external agencies is part of an ongoing process to up-skill and modernize the capacity of any B2B organization. Once the strategy and its implementation infrastructure are in place, the vast majority of functions will ideally be performed in-house, with specialist skills being provided by external partners.

The phases in our version of a Three Voices™ methodology comprise:

1. **Introductory phase**
2. **Project phase**
3. **Baseline phase**
4. **Aspiration phase**
5. **Strategy phase**
6. **Stakeholder discovery**
7. **Three Voices™ Engagement Landscape**
8. **Brand power-up**
9. **Three Voices™ Roadmap**
10. **Content Mechanics phase**
11. **Handover**

Each phase is described in more detail in the sections below, and can serve as a general guideline for your own Three Voices™ project.

1. The Introductory phase

Before any Three Voices™ strategic project can be planned, top management and other staff or business partners need to understand the big picture from a Three Voices™ perspective. This introduction can take the form of one or more formal presentations whose topics include:

- The evolution in B2B buyer behavior and the challenges and opportunities these changes present.

- The Three Voices™ strategic framework for meeting these challenges and realizing opportunities via three distinct modes of stakeholder engagement.

- Any available cases and insights that reveal the potential return on investment of a Three Voices™ strategy.

- How this initiative will support your company's stated business aims and strategy.

Since you will be seeking to change your company's fundamental approach to its market and other stakeholders—and because some degree of capital expenditure is required in the initial phases of the project—you will need to ensure the participation, understanding and motivated commitment of top management. Happily, our experience shows that many business leaders are highly interested in tuning their organizations to the needs of the market (becoming customer-centric), they understand and are inspired by Three Voices™ thinking, and that your message is likely to receive a warm welcome.

Once you have secured the attention and enthusiasm of management, you will need to conduct a more detailed assessment of the project, presenting the findings to obtain the official go-ahead. Issues to address include:

- What is the overarching pain point or area of opportunity to be addressed?

- What's the basic process and timing of this change?

- What resources are required to plan and implement such a strategy?

- What is the likely impact on the organization?

- Who's on the project team and who else is closely involved?

2. The Project phase

Once key decision-makers have announced their support for the project, it's time to get down to the details of:

- What will be done?
- Who will do it?
- Who will govern it?
- How to work together?
- What resources it will take?

At the beginning of the Project phase, you will need to gain a quick overview of the strategic landscape, forming a sketchy hypothesis about the nature of the changes you need to effect. Of course, there is much work to be done before you can definitively determine what should be done and what it will take to do it.

Project scoping

What's the development project's size, priority, likely budget range and significance within your organization? What are the expected benefits of this project to the organization? How will it change, help, protect, improve things? What will success look like? How will essential skills and tools be adopted by your organization and what tasks might be outsourced on an on-going basis?

Project organization

Discuss the staffing requirements for your project and how this group or groups should interact with key decision-makers inside and outside the organization to ensure the project's success. What are the reporting mechanisms? Who should be involved internally and externally? Can your current communication partners deliver what you need—or are they locked into more traditional ways of approaching B2B markets?

Project process and timeline

Match your needs to an overall Three Voices™ strategic implementation process, deciding which steps are applicable, when and to what level of detail. Then, with the process in place, map out a timeline for the project.

Project proposal

With the project's requirements firmly established, you should now produce a proposal that outlines decisions made so far, additional resources required and an estimate of the budget.

For now, focus on the desired outcome. Resist the temptation to spell out detailed descriptions of the project process or break down the elements that might be produced, as this can accurately be determined only once the project is well underway. Instead, aim to work out what funding, headcounts and man-hours may be required for the next two or three years, ask top management to commit to this level of effort, and decide on a plan that takes things a step at a time, determining exact deliverables in due course as the plan progresses.

This process reflects a fundamentally different approach from the old way of performing marketing tasks where marketers come up with a definitive answer to the task at hand, then exhaust all their resources creating a one-shot beast that could either succeed or fail (with little or no funding set aside for adjustments following its launch). Adopting the new approach may require a cultural shift in attitudes toward budgeting, particularly where external consultants are involved. Instead of playing cat and mouse with the details of your budget, you will need to be open about the resources available right from the beginning, trusting that everyone on the project will recommend the use of those funds as effectively as possible to ensure the company achieves its goals.

We believe a high level of trust between your company and its external partners is a pre-requisite for getting the best out of your Three Voices™ strategy. Only once this is in place can you establish a situation where you and your partners are firmly on the same team, openly sharing ideas and acknowledging realities with everyone focused on getting the best possible results with the least possible resources deployed.

With the project proposal in place, ensure that top management has read, accepted, and formally signed off on the project—after all, its outcome is likely to be key to the continued success of the company as a whole.

Project kick-off

We like to mark the beginning of what can, at times, be pretty hard work, with an informal kick-off event for the core team and, preferably, the steering committee and management sponsor, too. The exact form is flexible, from an evening dinner to christening the project with a bottle of good champagne at the office. The goal: to acknowledge the importance of the project, add to the team spirit among the project's members and begin the journey on a positive note.

3. The Baseline phase

For the Baseline phase of a Three Voices™ strategy you and your project partners should analyze both existing and new information extracted from your business. The goal is to arrive at a shared understanding of the current status of your company and its markets and identify where there may be potential for, or resistance to, new developments. For your external partners, this is a chance to dive into your industry, gaining expertise that will put them in a better position to advise you and deliver the best results.

Here's a quick overview of some of the factors you would be wise to cover during the Baseline phase:

General Industry assessment

Here you should examine broad market factors such as size, growth, profitability, trends, risk, competition, differentiation, value chains, stakeholders, segmentation, and more. Also consider the status and influence of thought leadership in the industry.

Company assessment

Now it's all about you. What's your business model? What are your growth aims? How do you intend to get there? Your history? Product portfolio and roadmap? Demand for each product? Differentiation? Quality? Brand equity? Marketing and communication resources and processes? What sorts of new products, concepts or other initiatives might support these aims? What threats do you face and what opportunities exist for you? Give plenty of attention to IP and subject matter expertise—they are important to understand at a general level although the specific strategic and tactical decisions regarding these will be explored in more depth further into the process.

Customer perspective

Focusing on your company's target markets, how do you segment your prospects and customers? How large is each segment? What is your market share in each segment? How do your offerings stack up against customer preferences and trends? How do your prospects and customers perceive your organization? Do you know who your ideal customers are? What else do they buy? What are their likes, dislikes, values? Their pain points and hot buttons?

The degree to which your Baseline phase is supported by "real" data gleaned via market research will depend on the resources you have available, the attitude of management toward such research and the project's timeline. While best guesses are likely to be useful—and are often all there is to go on—there is, however, some data you will need to provide with a higher degree of accuracy. But more about that shortly.

4. The Aspiration phase

Newcomers to the world of B2B business (or those recently promoted to a level where they can join strategic planning meetings) may be surprised to discover that many companies lack a clearly established and communicated business strategy. Often, what masquerades as corporate strategy is really just a collection of impressive-sounding vision statements, a few broadly stated directions and a list of revenue and profitability targets. That might not seem like an issue for companies whose marketing plan is equally vague and where the return on marketing investments is poorly measured, but it's a potential source of difficulty when working with targeted marketing approaches such as a Three Voices™ strategy.

We often find ourselves working with management to clarify the organization's market-oriented goals and the strategy to achieve them, working until everyone is on the same page about which specific initiatives to take and how success will be measured. After all, without clarity of purpose, it's difficult to design marketing and communication activities that can deliver strong and consistent results.

The Aspiration phase focuses on determining the business goals your Three Voices™ strategy should support, with the following phase, the Strategy phase, mapping out an overall plan for how to achieve these goals.

We recommend you arrive at a simple, but compelling description of where you want to take things in terms of an overall aspiration. One example of such an aspiration could be: "Leverage thought leadership to become the brand most often short-listed by our target customers." As a starting point for your Three Voices™ project, your aspiration may be very broad or somewhat more narrow, such as "improve our reputation among refrigeration engineers in the Brazilian market".

Below are a few examples of aspirations to help you work through the exercise:

Industry-level

- Establish a thought leadership position that puts your company at the center of industry conversations and increases your influence in standards committees.

- Convince the market that your new GSX technology should be widely adopted as the industry's de facto platform.

- Increase the perception of know-how as a key parameter in choosing a supplier.

Customer-level

- Cultivate an engaged group of prospects and customers who recommend your company to others.

- Be seen by your customers in Germany as dominating the local SME market for cloud-based CRM solutions.

Company-level

- Generate more than 2,000 leads (as defined by your pipeline process) a month one year after launch.

- Increase the number of quote requests by 300 percent within 12 months.

- Become recognized as a customer advocate instead of a sales-focused player.

- Establish your company as the industry's preferred place to work, particularly for software engineers in Europe.

Once you are clear on your overall goal, you're ready to determine the changes you hope to effect in the minds, hearts and habits of stakeholders through the staged implementation of a Three Voices™ strategy. You should also be ready to discuss with your project partners how to quantify and link KPIs to these aspirations, and to establish milestoned timelines for the achievement of your goals.

5. The Strategy phase

Now that you have identified what you want to achieve, and you have top management as well as the project team and steering committee on the same page, it's time to figure out how you are going to get there. Everyone will approach this task differently, but the key is to arrive at a focused, structured description of what will be done, converted into actionable and quantifiable measures.

In the Strategy phase, we typically conduct one or more workshops to translate the output of the Aspiration phase into a "big picture" strategic plan. For our work, we find a Strategic House model useful to sum up the strategic foundation, aims and initiatives.

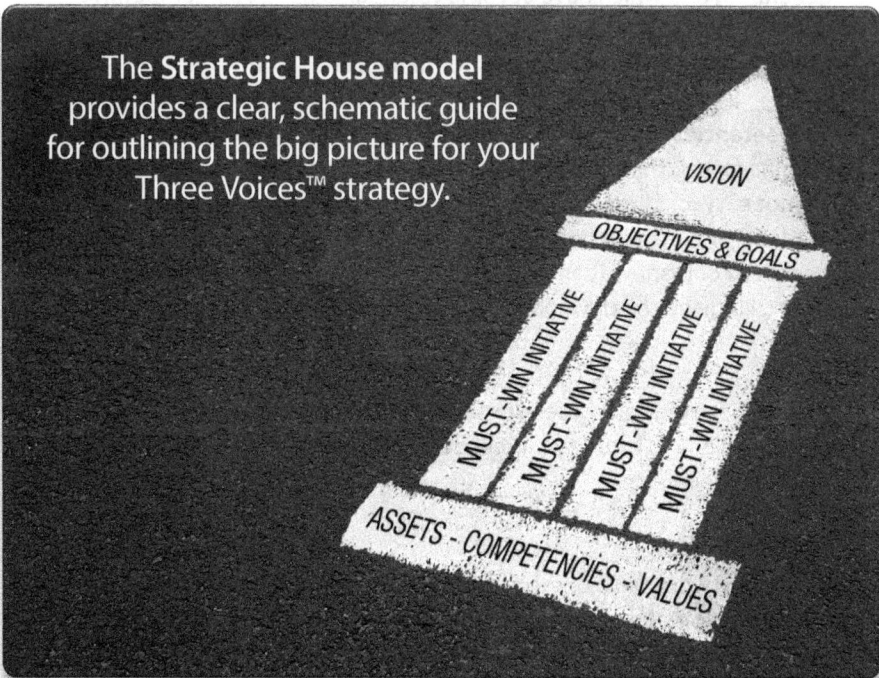

Figure 8.1 The Strategic House planning tool.

Building a Strategic House is a method of ensuring strategic clarity and, simultaneously, a simple way of communicating the strategy to internal audiences. The model helps the project team to avoid common planning errors such as the creation of siloed initiatives instead of synergistic ones. If you haven't worked with this type of model before, the creation of a Strategic House is probably something that is best accomplished using the services of an external facilitator. But, while performing the exercise demands masterly concentration and focus, we've found that the final product is hard to beat when it comes to providing a clear path for your Three Voices™ project.

We define the various components of a Strategic House as follows:

Assets
The set of goods, tangible or intangible, which the company has been generating and which have become essential to develop a competitive advantage in your market. For example, specialized machinery, patents, marks, know-how, databases of information, and so on.

Competencies
Specific factors that a business sees as central to the way it works. They are not easy for competitors to imitate, can be leveraged widely to many products and markets, and must contribute to the end user's experienced benefits. For Disney, as an example, core competencies might include storytelling and the development of iconic characters.

Values
A shared, strategically based sense of right and wrong or what "ought" to be—guiding attitudes and behavior, and ultimately, the company's success or failure.

Vision
By "Vision" we mean a one-sentence statement that translates the overall aspiration from the preceding Aspiration exercise into a clear strategic intent strongly related to your company's overall business aim.

Must-Win Initiatives
The three to five critical tasks most likely to make or break your ability to achieve success with your overall business strategy. An example could be "Convince the industry that GXS technology is best." Don't fall into the trap of creating too many of these—the more you have, the harder it is to arrive at an executable and communicable plan.

Objectives and goals

Here we turn each of your Must-Win Initiatives from headlines into solid, quantified aims.

So, for example, "Largest share of the Chinese market" becomes "At least RMB 2bn net sales run-rate by December 2012 at 15% margin". "Convince the industry GXS is the best technology" becomes "A 20% increase over benchmark in customers preferring GXS over STD by March 2014." With clarity like this, you can begin to delegate sub-goals, activities and responsibilities within your organization to make sure each of the Must-Win Initiatives succeeds.

By now, the original brief may have undergone some serious change—for the better. The project team now has a very clear understanding of what needs to be achieved, so it's time to adjust the formal brief to reflect these changes. Strategic revisions may also impact your ideas of who needs to be involved, what other aspects are likely to be influenced within and outside your organization, and what the implications may be for your overall business strategy and expectations.

The Strategy phase culminates, therefore, in a revised brief for your Three Voices™ project.

6. The Stakeholder Discovery phase

During the Baseline phase, you will already have drawn up a stakeholder map for your industry. This information, together with decisions made in the Strategy phase, will give you a good idea of which stakeholders merit your focused attention. Now you should be interested in learning more about the people whose attitudes and decisions influence the health and wealth of your company.

In the world of content marketing, which is the discipline we now enter, everything usually centers around the concept of buyer personas—a term that describes a relatively detailed profile of buyer types that helps the company to persuade such buyers to choose its products, services or solutions. For your Three Voices™ strategy, however you should think in terms of the company's wider audience of influencers, using the persona approach to develop and work with profiles of all stakeholders your company would like to influence.

So what steps might you take to define these personas? Below is a typical progression (with thanks to B2B content marketing advisor Barbra Gago for her input):

Identify stakeholder personas

How many personas you need is going to depend on the type of business you're in and the size and sophistication of your company. In B2B, decisions are often made by a group of people, so you may need several personas to represent those influencing the decision (as well as one or more of the final decision-makers).

Ultimately, determination of the level of complexity of your persona model is a data-driven cost/benefit equation. Given that most B2B companies aren't big on market research, this will typically be based on educated guesses and anecdotal feedback from the existing sales force.

- What services do your clients and prospects most want and need?
- What are the core strengths of your organization?
- How do people feel after they use your services?
- Where do your clients and prospects hang out?
- What are your customers trying to accomplish by using your products or services?
- Describe your typical customer (needs, desires, preferences, fears, pains…)
- What are the key words or phrases associated with those needs, desires and so on?
- Who do customers perceive as your competition?
- How do prospects find you?
- What are the central keywords and trigger words that your target audience might use to describe the key products and services or information you provide?

If you sell multiple products or services to different audiences, you'll need personas for each audience—or you will need to make choices that keep things operationally simple. Specific personas are needed for each of these groups because you need to engage with them differently.

As you go through this process, be sure to give each persona a real name—like Generous George or Careful Karen—making them more real and memorable for everyone who needs to keep them in mind. Even include a photo or illustration of each.

Prioritize your stakeholders

Ranking stakeholders helps to focus engagement, especially towards those who will be highly influential and highly impacted. Using a fairly simple stakeholder prioritization process can facilitate this ranking. Initially, aim to identify low-hanging fruit and map out a future path to develop links to high-value but difficult-to-target stakeholders such as CEOs.

Determine their issues

Once you have arrived at a number of target personas, it's time to identify questions they might have at each stage of the buying process. Initially, understanding these parameters will again be a case of educated guesswork but, as the process matures, the task should be increasingly data-driven.

For now, figure out what questions your personas have by asking your sales force, sampling customers or analyzing user/professional groups. If your budget stretches far enough, do secondary research (finding studies that already exist) or commission primary research yourself. Try to reduce the guesswork as much as possible by leveraging existing customer feedback loops (both qualitative and quantitative).

Determine answers to stakeholder issues

Once you have identified the most important questions related to each persona, you can start to construct a framework that includes questions, possible answers and even the most appropriate content types (such as FAQs, white papers, videos or even live online support). Identify which content formats are best suited to each stage of the sales cycle, and discover the most appropriate styles in which to provide your persona with the content—heavy-duty technical, or lighter, shorter pieces?

Match business objectives to each persona—what would you like them to do or think as a result of your communication? How will you get them to engage more closely (such as give you their email permission or subscribe to your newsletter). When is this best done? What does this mean for the types of content you create for that persona?

Perform a content audit

Now that you have an idea of the questions and issues likely to be raised by your personas at various stages of the buying cycle, it's time to figure out what content you ideally need to address these and how it might best be provided, ideally in the manner that's appropriate for specific usage—your salespeople, for example, might need PowerPoint presentations to support individual sales processes, while technical influencers at customer sites may prefer printed documentation.

Map content to issues

Map your existing content and knowledge to known industry issues. Think of this as industry knowledge hygienics—doing what everyone else is doing because you need to be seen to be playing the game, with a voice and opinion on the usual topics.

Identify content gaps

When you mapped existing content to the various persona and industry issues, where were the gaps? This is the sweet spot for your content marketing efforts. Specifically, you should be looking for gaps in the existing industry know-how that match company knowledge strengths (either existing or quickly developed). These gaps are an opportunity to create ownership, dictate the terms of industry knowledge and potentially frame the issues in support of your offerings. Use the gaps to re-define the market's "anchoring" buying criteria: the standard by which all other solutions will be judged in the mind of a buyer.

Determine content to be created

Based on the previous exercise, allocate your content creation resources over, for example, the next 12 months, on the basis of addressing either industry knowledge hygienics (the me-too stuff you just have to do) or hitting the sweet spot with what some content marketers call a Unique Knowledge Proposition.

Perform a Subject Expert audit

This is where the rubber meets the road—identifying exactly who can contribute the know-how you need to execute your thought leadership plans. It's time to think about who owns which subjects within the organization (or who likes to think they do). Keep an eye open for politics as you go since, in our experience, many experts build their position within the organization based on what they know, and they guard their knowledge with great pride. Assess the risks with key subject experts and evaluate what each person can reasonably be requested to contribute to the program. For example, what do you want to achieve with the more technical (and perhaps less easily understood) subject experts in terms of your stakeholder engagement plans?

Determine content types

As you develop content, you should be constantly looking out for topics and issues that capture each persona's attention, and their preferred content formats at different stages in the buying cycle. Knowing how your target audiences like to consume information will increase the likelihood that they will engage with your company's content.

7. Building a Three Voices™ engagement landscape

Before determining the types of content and style we will create for our various buyer personas, we need to consider the media options we can use to communicate our messages and engage in dialogue. It's not a task to be underestimated, as any seasoned marketer will know, and with all the options available to today's B2B companies it seems to be getting tougher by the day. To make the job easier, it is useful to think in terms of a landscape for your Three Voices™ activities.

Remember the old movie scenes where a group of high-ranking, handlebar-moustached officers are grouped around a large table, each armed with a small wooden rake? On the table is a map of a battle area. Every now and then, they use the rake to push small ships, tanks or troops around on the table. The idea, of course, is to create a clear and actionable overview of the situation. And that's precisely what we have discovered is missing from many B2B marketing departments. Instead of having a clear idea of the options available, and basing choices on a previously determined strategy, marketers often fall into the trap of launching campaigns in a haphazard fashion. Choices are often made on the basis of what comes immediately to mind, and potential opportunities or synergies may be overlooked.

Inspired by war tables and war rooms, we set out to create a chart that laid out the battlefield from a media perspective. You use this Three Voices™ Landscape chart to take any particular conversation they are about to have with the market (such as the launch of a new product or the highlighting of an industry-level issue) and consider where that conversation should take place and how its content elements should be distributed in terms of owned, earned and paid media options. Figure 8.2 shows an example of such a Three Voices™ Landscape seen from a Voice of Industry perspective.

To create a chart like this, you need to have good insight and skills in the planning of content distribution. You will also need to make some informed choices about which options are relevant for your particular circumstances. Importantly, there are also generalizations to be made when it comes to sorting out what you consider to be owned, earned or paid media. While there are no absolute and unarguable answers to whether, for example, YouTube is owned or earned media, we have found the following guidelines useful for creating an actionable Three Voices™ Landscape:

Owned media—sites and contexts that are your property, under your control to the extent that the rules of the game are dictated by your company and not by other entities. You must also own the data itself—not just the content, but all the data on, and access permissions to, users of that content. For example, a website or an in-person seminar series you've developed as a company falls into this category, while YouTube or LinkedIn activities do not.

Earned media—we define this category as encompassing any media for which you need to earn your way to a presence—whether that is in terms of creating content so compelling that other bloggers, news sites or similar are keen to use it, or by having to apply manhours and money to create your presence as in the case of LinkedIn, Facebook or Google+.

Paid media—the essential idea of paid media is that you can, with a reasonable degree of probability, order and pay for a specific amount of attention from a specific audience. And this is the definition we use to place banner advertising, Adwords, trade ads and so on under the paid media category.

As you construct your Three Voices™ Landscape, it's worth remembering that your activities with paid and earned media should be thought of as bait put out to lure prospects and customers to your owned media platforms where the real power lies for your long-term stakeholder engagement capabilities. If your company has already built its marketing presence purely on earned media, look to move the main part of your activities to owned media platforms. Why? Just look at the direction that earned media such as Facebook are taking—namely, increasing their own access to and control over the audiences of those who have chosen to use the site's services. Overnight, what you may have thought were your own assets could be hijacked by your host's own and possibly conflicting commercial agenda.

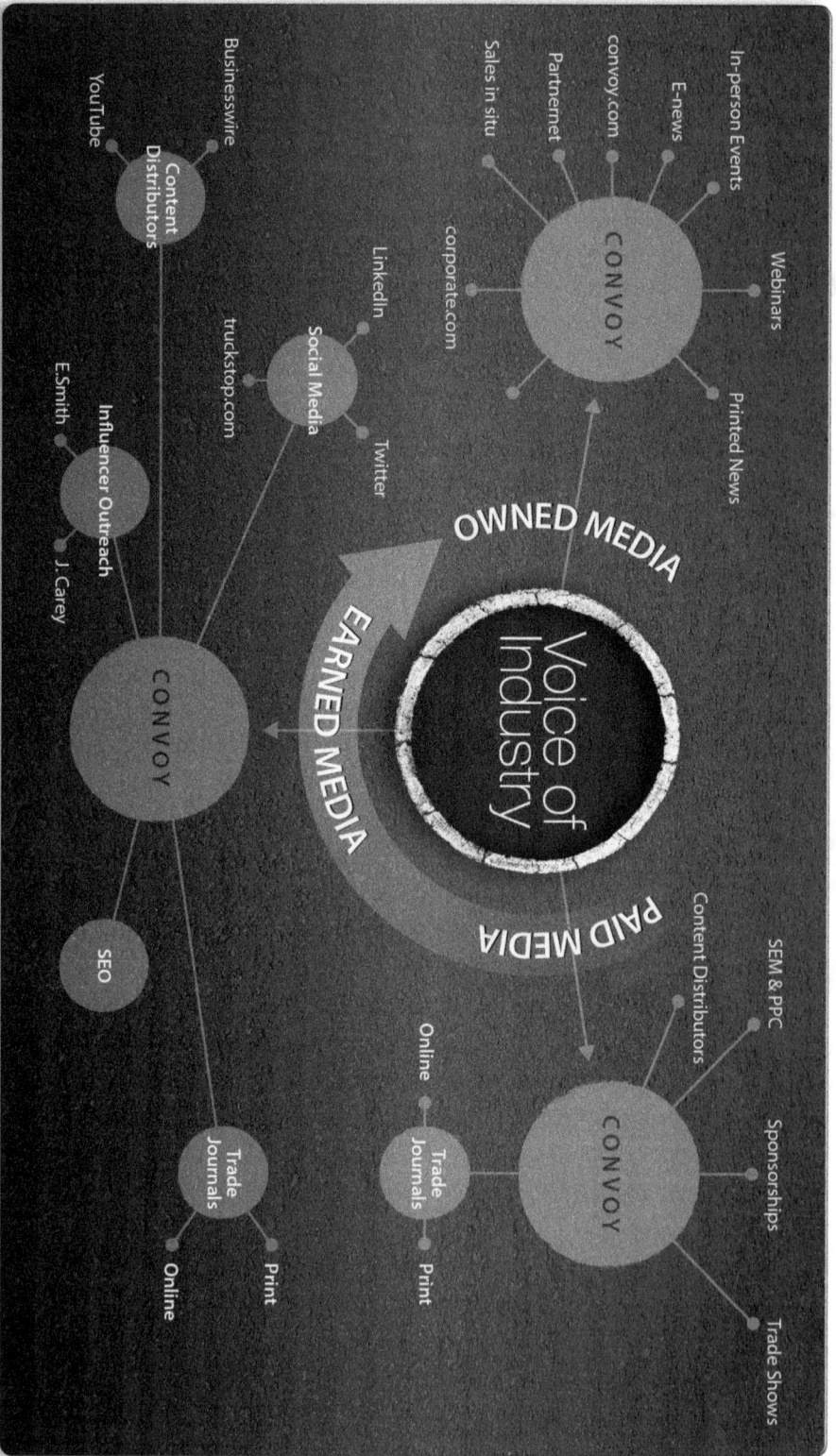

Figure 8.2 A fictitious truck manufacturer's Three Voices™ Landscape, laying out its Voice of Industry playing field. For this example, the company's VOI activities are gathered under an industry-level creative concept called "Convoy".

8. The Brand Power-up phase

As we touched upon earlier, for most companies there's work to be done to put their Voice of Company in order before the full potential of a Three Voices™ strategy can be realized:

- Reduce or eliminate progaganda.

- Express your value proposition/s with clarity and impact.

- Develop a strong brand story and identity—with an emotional connection.

Few B2B companies will have the in-house skills required to properly perform these important tasks. Working with your ad agency or other communication partners (if they are skilled in content marketing) will achieve the best result.

There's another aspect to working with your Voice of Company that is likely to require time and budget. That's the task of preparing your corporate website to add distribution power to Voice of Industry content. For example, a new white paper created around an industry issue should ideally be promoted on your corporate site, encouraging people to visit your Voice of Industry platform, explore content on the site and download the paper, register as members or take some other form of action. To do this, you may have to change the way, for example, that your homepage highlights such items.

9. The Three Voices™ Roadmap

Now that you have identified the types of content most likely to attract the attention of your stakeholders, as well as which media you will emphasize when distributing this content, it's time to begin planning your first campaigns.

For most of our clients, executing a content-driven marketing strategy is something quite new. They seldom have the appropriate skillsets in house and their stakeholder engagement manager (we typically advise clients to hire a focused employee to help set up and operate their Three Voices™ strategy) also has much to learn. For this reason, we concentrate on providing a clear plan for content, media and interactions over the initial 12 months, translating these activities into required systems and resources that identify (for management and implementation staff) what is required of them during the period. The tool we use is known as a Three Voices™ Roadmap. Figure 8.3 depicts a fictitious example of a simple Roadmap with three campaigns planned to be rolled out over a 12-month period.

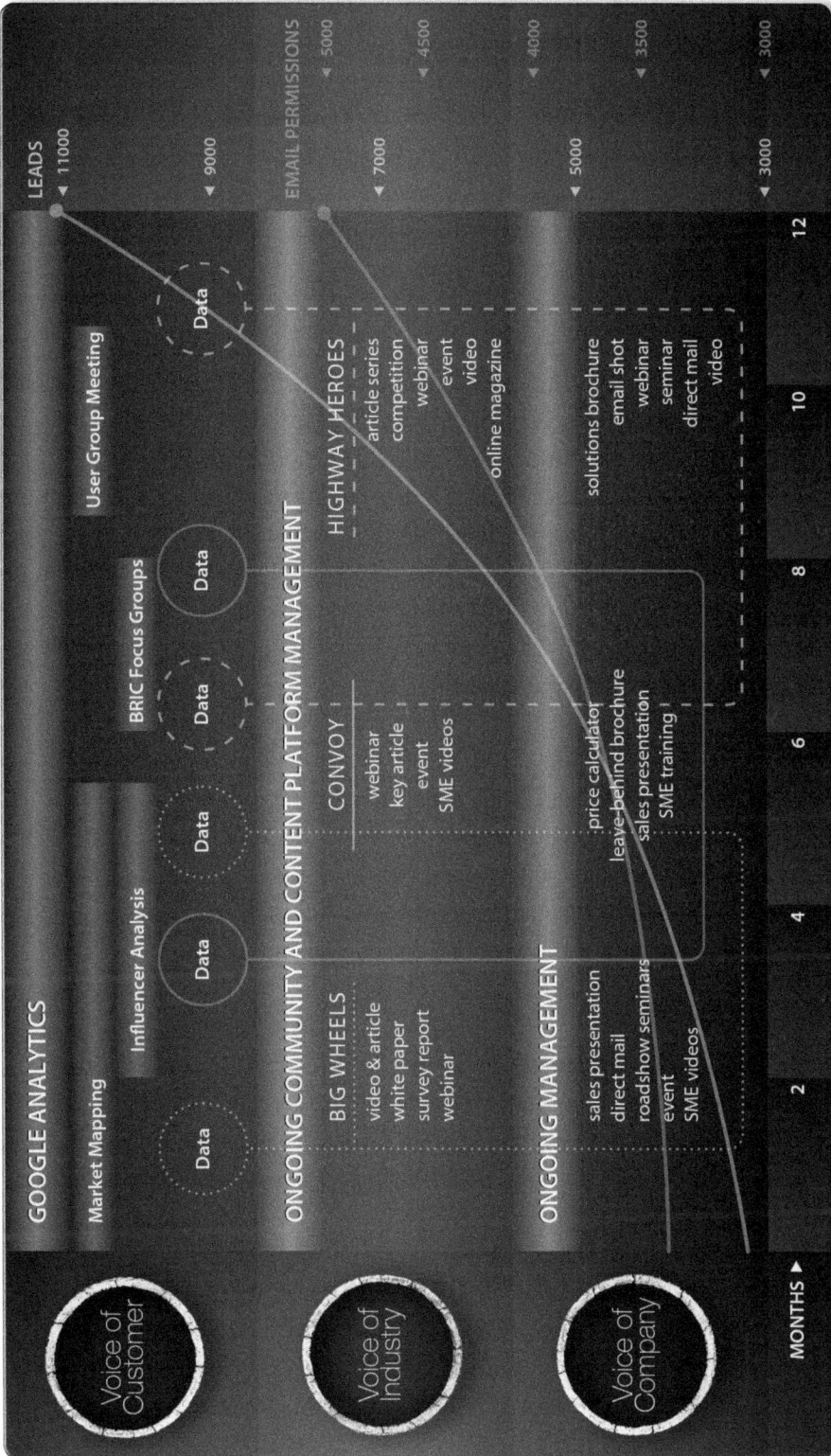

Figure 8.3 *A Three Voices™ Strategy Roadmap for our fictitious truck manufacturer.*

Roadmap Layer 1: Voice of Customer

The top layer of your Roadmap, labeled Voice of Customer, outlines the listening (and responding where appropriate) activities you plan to implement. Voice of Customer activities are divided into two parts: first, activities that are on-going, helping the company to learn useful general facts about its key markets; and second, activities that are campaign-focused, providing data that can help with campaign design and accuracy before launch, as well as following up after each campaign to assess its effect.

Our example is that of a truck manufacturer early on the Three Voices™ learning curve. Before any activity begins, the company plans to conduct basic market mapping to help it determine the viability of various market segments—and how to access and influence buyers in these segments. The company will also implement a comprehensive Google Analytics solution, and plans to deploy a social media listening tool to help discover and follow key influencers in its industry as they start or contribute to conversations on social media. Each of the three campaigns depicted in the layer below have pre-launch and follow-up data gathering as an integral element.

Roadmap Layer 2: Voice of Industry

The second layer, labeled Voice of Industry, shows the conversations (campaigns) you plan to conduct with your stakeholders at a Voice of Industry level during the period—and the individual items of content and activities you will produce and distribute to deliver the various parts of each conversation.

Roadmap Layer 3: Voice of Company

The layer beneath Voice of Industry depicts your company's Voice of Company with its various content items and marketing or sales activities. Here your focus should be on the interplay and possible synergies between Voice of Industry and Voice of Company elements.

While you are planning all of this, it's worth remembering that, in the new world of marketing, such plans are just a starting point rather than an enduring blueprint. Built-in Voice of Customer and KPI monitoring processes will provide early feedback that you should use to refine your Roadmap along the way.

Once you have roughly outlined the three layers of a Three Voices™ Roadmap, it's time to stand back and ask yourself some important questions, such as:

- Are we trying to do too much? Or too little?
- Can we realistically implement all of these activities?
- Is the sales force properly connected to our plan?
- Is there adequate coordination between, for example, the KPIs related to activities we are planning and the tools we will have in place at the time for measuring results?

If you're satisfied with the refined Roadmap, then it's time to begin building the machine that will produce, manage and optimize your content—a process we call the Content Mechanics Phase.

10. The Content Mechanics Phase

A question we meet at almost every client meeting to discuss the implementation of a Three Voices™ strategy goes something like this: "How can we produce enough good content to make a real difference?" To many, it seems like an almost impossible task—and one which is likely to delay the company's entry into the new world of content-driven marketing. Even to those in the know, it takes careful planning and no small amount of experience to know what to think about and what it takes to build a "content machine".

As you might imagine, it would take far too long to describe all of the elements of a corporate content machine in this book, so we will simply provide a list for now that alerts you to many of the issues you will need to think through before launching your Three Voices™ strategy.

People

- Content team, roles and responsibilities
- Internal training requirements
- Outsourcing and partnering strategy

Processes

- Content creation and maintenance strategy
    - Re-purposing and extension plan
    - Content approval workflows
    - Meta-data strategy
    - Localization plan
    - Personalization strategy
    - Formats guide
    - SEO strategy
    - Content maintenance plan

- Internal engagement strategy
    - Subject matter experts program

- External engagement strategy
    - Influencer strategy
    - CRM and permissions strategy

- Continuous improvement strategy
    - Measurement plan
    - Reporting plan

Tools & infrastructure

- Technology toolkit
- Content templates
- Backup and archiving system

Policies

- Legal compliance
- Privacy and security policies
- Content style guide
- Social media guidelines

An experienced content marketing agency will be able to provide guidance for this task, along with general rules of thumb to assist your resource planning. As part of our own work for clients, we also like to document each aspect of the company's content mechanics, providing a comprehensive overview of the new marketing system that can be used to bring new employees up to speed quickly, inform external partners or simply to maintain consistency for the system as a whole.

Once it's all in place, it is time to start rolling out the elements of your newly developed Three Voices™ Roadmap.

Planning your first campaign

We don't intend to delve too deeply into all the things you will need to consider when planning your first Voice of Industry conversations with your market—but we do want to discuss a few basic points that, despite their fundamental nature, are often missed by B2B marketers and communicators whose careers have taken a more traditional path.

The first of these points concerns campaign goals. In our conversations with B2B companies, we find that a lot of emphasis is (rightly) placed on the results of any activity. That's great. But since your company will no longer be judging the success or failure of an activity on the basis of the CEO's opinion or favorable comments from a few key customers, and because the return on marketing investments is about to become far more transparent, you will need to sharpen up on the data your company uses to allocate its marketing spend.

In the highly data-driven world of Three Voices™ strategy, identifying clear KPIs is an unavoidable step—and delivery on these KPIs is broadly measurable. The problem we often see, however, is that inexperienced marketers are all too quick to state goals for these KPIs without having done their data-gathering legwork first. For example, an executive from one company recently came under pressure from his management to set ambitious targets for the company's first Voice of Industry campaign results. Numbers of visitors to the core site and percentages of downloads were bandied about, much of the goal-setting process based on what might sound good or at least acceptable to management.

As we began to ask questions, it became clear that the company, not having conducted sufficient market research, knew very little about the audience it was trying to reach. For example, there were no figures on the number of companies in each geographic region, and almost no data on the number of various buyer types in each company. Without data on the number of CTOs in any one region—or an assumption about how many of them a) visited the media channels the company had decided to use, or b) were even able to understand English—accurately estimating the potential number of page views, unique visitors and leads generated for the campaign was simply impossible.

Of course, we're not saying that you must have comprehensive market research in place with all the required data before you can launch a campaign, but it's important to recognize the limitations of acting without sufficiently accurate information to support the determination of your campaign's direction and its stated goals. That said, we acknowledge that you have to walk before you can run—so start with the best information you have and focus on ways to gather more and better data over time.

You will need to develop a number of processes and tools for managing and communicating about your campaigns. For example, we have found it useful to use a specific tool for planning and presenting content strategies to management around a product launch or some other form of conversation with stakeholders.

11. The Handover phase

As you work through your Three Voices™ strategy project, you should begin to develop a clear plan of which skills and tools you would like to establish as in-house capabilities during or by the end of the project, and which capabilities will be outsourced for the foreseeable future. If you've commissioned external partners to help you develop your Three Voices™ strategy and the infrastructure that supports it, now it's time for them to help you recruit and train any staff you may wish to add (in addition to any employees that may have been recruited from the beginning of the project). You should, of course, expect that there will be a number of specialist skills that are best provided by agencies or freelancers that focus on these areas.

With everything in place, from strategy to staff to outsourcing, you should now be ready to expand your market reach, generate leads, uncover the real needs of prospective buyers, and harness the many benefits to be gained from a comprehensive Three Voices™ strategy.

Key take-outs

There are many ways to approach the planning and implementation of a Three Voices™ strategy. Each will have its own benefits, challenges and learning curve.

For example, our own version of a Three Voices™ implementation methodology comprises 11 phases:

- **Introductory**—top management and other key stakeholders need to understand the big picture from a Three Voices™ perspective, embracing the need for change and gaining an overview of the benefits that can be achieved and the steps required.

- **Project**—effective planning will help you determine what will be done, who will do it, who will govern it, and what resources it will take.

- **Baseline**—assessing the industry as a whole, your company and the customer perspective, the goal is to arrive at a deep understanding of where things are right now for your company and its markets.

- **Aspiration**—defining the business goals your Three Voices™ strategy should support allows you to determine the overall changes you hope to effect in the minds, hearts and habits of stakeholders.

- **Strategy**—via structured strategic thinking, the aim is to arrive at a focused description of what will be done, converted into actionable and quantifiable measures.

- **Stakeholder Discovery**—develop detailed stakeholder "personas" to engage and influence the people whose attitudes and decisions are important to your company.

- **Three Voices™ Landscape**—create a clear and actionable overview of the media options available, including content sharing partnerships, to communicate your messages and engage in dialogue, considering owned media, paid media and earned media.

- **Brand Power-up**—there's work to be done to get the Voice of Company in order before the full potential of a Three Voices™ strategy can be realized.

- **Three Voices™ Roadmap**—create a clear plan for content, media and interactions over a defined period, translating these activities into required systems and resources.

- **Content Mechanics**—consider the people, processes, tools, infrastructure and policies you need to create, distribute and monitor content and engagement.

- **Handover**—decide upon a clear plan of which skills and tools should be established as in-house capabilities and which capabilities will be outsourced, and recruit or train your existing staff accordingly.

Notes

Fight the Fear
and Do it Anyway

What's required to successfully introduce a Three Voices™ strategy to your company? First, the corporate will and commitment to do so. That typically requires a champion—perhaps a certain someone who has read this book and understands the transformative nature of a Three Voices™ approach to business strategy. In this last chapter, we touch briefly on topics of corporate culture, organizational structure and risk. In truth, each of these areas demands far closer examination than we can provide here, signalling key directions for the further development of Three Voices™ strategic thinking for the near future.

Toward a new way of being

Is your company culture closed to the new breed of B2B buyers? We've talked a lot about the way B2B buyers have become increasingly skeptical of corporate marketing and communications messages—and the move B2B vendors need to make away from "propaganda" toward "dialogue". And we've used words like "honesty", "openness" and "sharing" to describe the atmosphere that needs to underpin this dialogue. Finally, we have discussed the fact that there are many conversations going on about your industry and your own products, services and corporation to which you are not even invited. Which means, like being at a cocktail reception, you need to have something valuable to say every time or people will drift off to find another conversation partner.

All this has significant implications for the style in which B2B marketers and communicators approach their audiences. And frankly, not many corporations are necessarily ready for words like honesty, openness and sharing—at least, not when it comes to the way they promote themselves to external audiences! Instead, the company propaganda machine is still busily churning out carefully crafted statements and slogans designed to impress and dazzle B2B buyers into making a purchase. Allowing prospects and customers to engage in a more open and frank manner with the company, admitting mistakes or just saying "thanks" for an idea created in a public forum lies far from the typical corporate mindset.

The first to change corporate culture to match rapidly evolving markets were, of course, B2C or B2B+B2C companies. That's not to say that there are many of them that have gone the whole way to becoming Honest Jim, your regular next-door neighbor, in their style. But there is a noticeably greater degree of openness and straight talking in Steve Jobs' product introductions or the philanthropic participation of Google employees in the good of the communities in which they live.

> Few companies have incorporated openness and honesty into their marketing campaigns as strongly as Domino's Pizza, which ran an electronic ticker in Times Square during mid-2011 that displayed consumer opinions about the brand in real time. While profanities and anti-social statements were filtered out, all customer comments, whether good, bad or somewhere in between were revealed on a giant billboard. Inputs came from Domino's Tracker system, which enables customers to follow their orders. Integrated with new TV commercials, the campaign is further evidence of the company's repeated experience that transparency has a direct and positive effect on its image and sales.

Many successful medium-to-large sized companies were born with an engineering background. And while engineers in the R&D department can be so relaxed and open that it has some of our marketing director clients tearing their hair out, once they make it to top management, something seems to change. They get awfully protective of their knowledge and their "serious" corporate image.

In the words of B2B marketing commentator Chris Koch:

"Filtered conversation reduces risk. The ultimate risk in business is that your customers stop buying from you because they don't trust you. Preventing employees from speaking to customers because they might make a mistake ignores this much bigger risk—which existed long before social media came along. Customers want to speak to the people they will be working with. That's why employees and subject matter experts should be on the front lines of social media rather than marketers or PR people."

The new breed of B2B buyers do care about the cultural attitude displayed by their vendors. And they will increasingly support companies that show they are able to participate in industry conversations without hiding behind a stiff and lifeless corporate mask.

What does your own company's culture say to today's B2B buyers? Is it a match made in heaven or does something fundamental need to happen within your organization to get back on the right track?

How helping others helps you, too

Here's another corporately unfashionable value that your company will need to adopt in order to compete for the attention of the new breed of B2B buyer: the idea that, by helping others to achieve what they need to, you will be better able to achieve your own aims.

What really drives today's B2B customers is receiving help to achieve the goals that have been set by or for them. If you can be seen to help them, they'll buy your products and services. Of course, the kind of help we're talking about isn't just about products and services. You can also help people by recognizing them or supporting their careers (for example, by promoting their achievements and widening their personal web footprints on your Voice of Industry platform).

By thinking first and foremost about how to help B2B buyers (and KOLs or other potential business partners), you are starting off on the right foot— dropping a pushy sales pitch in favor of a more solution-oriented approach.

That's essentially the same style recommended by tried-and-proven best practice sales methodologies such as "spin selling" or "solution selling". It results in more open, trusting conversations about the buyer's true needs and challenges, leading to strategic partnerships between your company and your customers. And it can win you respect and strong connections in the marketplace instead of repeated rejection.

There's no reward without risk

Yes, there are risks when you decide to step out in the customer's world and start engaging with them. In fact, a survey of global marketers by Powerreviews and the e-tailing group (Community and Social Media Study, September 2009) identified the following as the three biggest fears of marketers contemplating the social space:

Brand degradation fear
People can trash my products in front of large audiences.

Competence fear
I am using outdated marketing/merchandising techniques.

Competitive fear
I'm afraid that customers will leave my site to find a more socially-engaging site.

As it happens, *Ayelet Noff*, founder and CEO of *Blonde 2.0*, discussed and dismissed those concerns in a very effective blog entry:

When you open a business and start marketing your services and exposing your brand to others, people will start talking about your brand. And this is why you exposed them to your brand in the first place.

People are going to be talking about your brand no matter what. The question is: Do you want to be a part of the dialogue or do you want to just play ostrich and ignore what people are saying? If a person is dissatisfied with your services, do you prefer he opens up this discussion in a "I hate <your brand>" group opened up by another hater or do you prefer that he come to your page and post the complaint there allowing you to respond appropriately and even perhaps win him back as a client?

Social media didn't create the dissatisfied customer—it only allowed him a platform to express his frustration. If you don't give him the stage to speak, he will do it elsewhere and it will cause a great deal more damage to your brand if you're not there to respond and open to criticism.

When we speak of social media, we speak of conversational marketing— listening before selling, opening a dialogue with the user and not just throwing a blinking banner in his face. Brands need to make that switch in their heads and understand that social media is SOCIAL. Many conversations will be positive and you will have these nice messages recorded for everyone to see publicly—your bosses, your investors, your customers and potential customers:

Some conversations may be negative but these conversations should be seen as welcomed opportunities to gain back customers. If you utilize social media effectively and are alert to what people are saying about you online, then you can also respond in a timely and intelligent manner. When you're dazed and confused and too afraid to see what people may be saying about you, that's when the conversation can get out of control and your branding and positioning can go out the window. Companies who understand social media know that by using social media they are increasing the number of positive responses to their brand and making sure to control and decrease the negative responses by showing people that they actually care about what they have to say.

In other words, yes, they're going to be talking about you—and sometimes those words will not be kind. Get over it. Focus instead on being insanely passionate about what you do and what your company produces—and ensure that your organization delivers products and services that match your enthusiasm. You'll soon win over the critics.

The structure

It pays to get the overall structure of your Three Voices™ strategy right from the beginning. One of the chief considerations relates to the way activities are structured within the organization. Look to create an easily scalable structure that can exist and grow in a way that suits the way your company works—its reporting structures, budgets, human capital and culture. We find it useful to consider how organizations have tended to structure their social media activities and to apply similar structures to the broader offline and online activity sphere of a Three Voices™ strategy.

In many cases, companies that have been running social media activities for some time have moved beyond individual silos of activity to an organization-wide structure that achieves a better result than the sum of its parts. Determining that structure involves thinking about a number of common choices as discussed by the industry analyst Jeremiah Owyang during his keynote speech at the BazaarVoice conference in 2011:

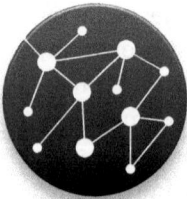

Decentralized—used with success by Sun Microsystems, decentralized structures usually grow organically, experimentally and with a minimum of coordination. Authenticity and credibility are typically high due to the "grass roots" nature of such structures.

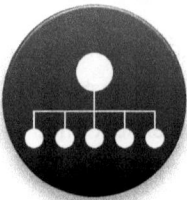

Centralized—a centralized structure is where one department controls all efforts and is typically used by companies seeking to exert maximum control over social media activities. Credibility is usually more difficult to achieve, as the corporate orchestration is difficult to hide from your audiences. Consistency is higher, risk may in some cases be easier to deal with, but you should expect correspondingly less authenticity and enthusiasm within your organization.

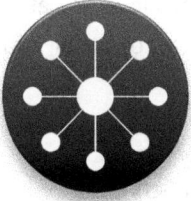

Hub and Spoke—in this model, a central hub sets the rules and procedures for the use of social media in the organization as a whole, while individual business units apply these guidelines to undertake their own efforts. This type of structure takes time to mature but spreads widely around the organization. The Red Cross uses such a structure.

Multiple Hub and Spoke or "Dandelion"—used by companies such as Hewlett-Packard, this structure is an expanded version of the Hub and Spoke model, but is based around multiple brands and business units.

Holistic or "Honeycomb"—the Holistic structure is essentially decentralized, but empowers each employee under a clear set of guidelines. Intel, Dell and Best Buy deploy their social media via this type of structure.

The people

By now, you may be fretting that the whole Three Voices™ approach requires a large-scale commitment in terms of staffing—resources that you may not be able to spare just now.

Rest easy. Again, let's draw upon the approaches of companies who have introduced social media and extrapolate their efforts to a Three Voices™ strategy. A recent study by H. James Wilson, PJ Guinan, Salvatore Parise and Bruce D. Weinberg (quoted in Harvard Business Review July/August 2011) suggests that companies operating effectively in the social space could be classified at one of four levels, each requiring different resources (from little to rather a lot):

Predictive practitioners
This is the first step on the ladder. Companies at this level typically confine their efforts to a single discipline, such as Customer Service or New Product Development. Household products company Clorox is an example, using Voice of Company social initiatives for virtual R&D. The company created *Clorox Connects*, a website that enables brainstorming with customers and suppliers.

Creative experimenters
Companies at this level operate on a slightly broader canvas, conducting small-scale tests that might occur within any part of the organization, but which are deliberately contained in scope and duration. IT services giant EMC created its own internal social media platform, EMC/ONE to help relatively new employees network and connect on projects. "We were very clear that in two months we might unplug this and try a completely different approach," said EMC director of social strategy Len Devanna. "This was the reason we were inside the firewall: to be free to make mistakes and learn our lessons before exposing ourselves to the outside."

Social media champions
Companies at this level typically commission large initiatives in social media for predictable results. A typical example was the Ford Motor Company's 2009 "Fiesta Movement" campaign, launching the new model into the U.S. This campaign, lending cars to bloggers and other social media influencers for six months, required close collaboration across marketing, communications and the C-suite, and delivered massive exposure and engagement for a five million dollar investment. The campaign was never intended, nor was it likely, to change the company's culture.

Social media transformers
Organizations who make it to this level invest in large-scale interactions that extend to external stakeholders, allowing companies to use the unexpected to improve the way they do business. In 2010, Cisco launched Integrated Work Experience (IWE), a social business platform designed to facilitate internal and external collaboration and decentralize decision-making. One manager likens it to Amazon: "IWE makes recommendations based on what you are doing, the role you are in and the choices of other people like you. We are basically allowing appropriate information to find you."

Skills required

The more involved your Three Voices™ program is, the greater the range of skills that will be required. In the early days, however, most of the work can be handled from within the organization or in tandem with existing suppliers. As your needs become more complex, however, you'll need to engage with a number of new contributors (including an unfamiliar role or two).

You'll need to contract with, employ or redeploy staff as:

- Developers
- Writers
- Editors
- Researchers
- Social customer support staff
- Community managers

You'll know (or be able to figure out) most of those roles—but the last one may be new to many. Let's explore the role of community manager in a little more detail.

Stakeholder Engagement Manager: The hottest new job in integrated B2B marketing and communication

So you've optimized your website for the new breed of B2B buyer, you've built your industry content site and you have the beginnings of a social network that will enable conversations among your prospective customers, customers and other industry. What's more, you're putting the finishing touches on a well thought-out content strategy. Congratulations—you're well on the way to communicating the way today's B2B buyers like it. If you're not careful, however, now is when it can (almost) all fall apart.

A large Scandinavian manufacturer with multiple business units knows just what we mean. Its corporate communications department set up ten separate online communities, one for each of the major business areas. The idea was, of course, that employees, in particular, would flock to the communities and their enthusiasm for the new means of knowledge-sharing would turn the communities into a thriving business enabler. But just the opposite happened. Within a short time, the company's investment in social networking lay in ruins, each community akin to a classic ghost town, just without the tumbleweed.

What they were missing, of course, was a "stakeholder engagement manager" (or similar job title). This person is fast becoming one of the most sought-after employee profiles in the marketing and communication business. What does a stakeholder engagement manager do exactly? Think of your B2B marketing and communication platform as a newly planted garden. It needs regular care and attention, not too much and not too little watering, as well as the right type and amount of fertilizer at the right moments. So what you need is, in fact, an experienced gardener.

A word of warning, however: don't think that someone with years of experience writing code for social networks is able to fill the boots of a community manager. It's much more important to find a person who knows the value of content and who understands what gets people to join, use and stay loyal to online social networks. You need this person to help you get the strategy right first, then to assist with implementation afterward, preferably using external developers to do the coding.

People like that, however, don't grow on trees. And right now, there are few training courses available for such a role. In the meantime, marketers may be able to strike a deal with a community-savvy communications agency, hiring its services on a retainer basis to help you get off on the right foot. Such an agency could also help to train a staff member to the point where that person could take over many of the outsourced community manager's core tasks.

If a full-on Three Voices™ strategic planning process seems like too much for you right now, then we offer another piece of advice: just get started! Don't spend too much time thinking about the big picture of it all, because you probably won't have any idea what sorts of things your stakeholders will react best to until you have actually started putting some activities in place. Whatever you do, don't delay—it could cost you much more in lost business.

Here's one way to get started without breaking the bank or limiting your choices as your strategy evolves to the next level: create a periodically published, online or offline magazine that can serve as your initial Voice of Industry platform. Once you begin to see initial results from the Voice of Industry program (see the ROI benchmarking program recommended in this book), you will have some solid data to argue your case for sufficient budget to commit to a Three Voices™ strategy on a rather larger scale.

Need more convincing? Head back to Page One and start again.
Before you go, though, one more thing…

The Beginning (of your Three Voices™ journey)

Start small.

Make some mistakes.

Find some champions from within.

Make them heroes.

And above all else, start engaging with your customers.
They're dying to have some real conversations.

Key take-outs

- Organizational structure, people and money are essential considerations when developing a Three Voices™ strategy.

- Structural choices include Decentralized, Centralized, Hub and Spoke, Multiple Hub and Spoke, and Holistic.

- With more and more businesses jumping onto the Voice of Industry bandwagon, more funds need to be allocated to producing sufficient quantities of engaging content.

- The more involved your organization becomes with your Three Voices™ program, the greater the range of skills that will be required.

- The new role of "stakeholder engagement manager" will be crucial to the success of your new activities.

- If a full Three Voices™ strategic planning process is too much to bite off right now, look for a way to get started—perhaps via a Voice of Industry offline or online magazine.

Notes

Bibliography

Baer, Jay and Amber Naslund. <u>The NOW Revolution: 7 Shifts to Make Your Business Faster, Smarter and More Social</u>. John Wiley & Sons, 2011.

Black, Leyl Master. "4 Tips for B2B Marketing on Facebook." Mashable Business article. May 20, 2010. <http://mashable.com/2010/05/20/facebook-b2b-tips/>.

Brownlow, Mark. "31 content tips and ideas for your B2B email newsletter." Email Marketing Reports. October 2006. <http://www.email-marketing-reports.com/newsletters/content.htm>.

Burnes, Rick. "Social Media Monitoring in 10 Minutes a Day." HubSpot. March 10, 2010.

Carlsson, Christian C. "Ratings and Reviews for the Business User." June 16, 2008.

Creative Commons. <http://creativecommons.org/>.

Deckers, Erik. Reader comment on Smaller Indiana forum. August 14, 2008. <http://www.smallerindiana.com/forum/topics/1736855:Topic:133406>.

Ducharme, Jim. "Olivier Blanchard: Practical Social Media ROI." Fusion Marketing Experience article. April 21, 2011. <http://www.fusionmarketingexperience.com/2011/04/olivier-blanchard-practical-social-media-roi/>.

Elliot, Nate. "The Easiest Way to a First-Page Ranking on Google." Forrester Blogs. January 8, 2009. <http://blogs.forrester.com/interactive_marketing/2009/01/the-easiest-way.html>.

Flitter, Justin. "Big Brand Kiwi Retailers - Where Are You?" Voxy blog. February 20, 2010. <http://www.voxy.co.nz/business/big-brand-kiwi-retailers-where-are-you/1242/39167>.

Fugere, Brian. "Movies with a message: Deloitte employees unleash their inner director and make the company's first-ever film festival a success." Communication World. January 1, 2009.

Gago, Barbra. "4 Questions Answered about Buyer Personas." Content Marketing Institute article. April 13, 2011. <http://www.contentmarketinginstitute.com/2011/04/4-questions-answered-about-buyer-personas/>.

Gitomer, Jeffrey. Social BOOM! How to Master Business Social Media. FT Press, 2011.

Gladwell, Malcolm. The Tipping Point. Little, Brown and Company, 2000.

Gutsell, Catherine. "Join the social club." The HR Director feature article. August 18, 2011. <http://www.thehrdirector.com/features/social-media/join-the-social-club>.

Halvorson, Kristina and Melissa Rach. Content Strategy for the Web. 2nd ed. New Riders. 2012

Hibbard, Casey. "How Social Media Helped Cisco Shave $100,000+ Off a Product Launch." Social Media Examiner article. August 30, 2010. <http://www.socialmediaexaminer.com/cisco-social-media-product-launch/>.

Koch, Chris. "15 things marketers should stop doing and thinking in 2011." Idea Marketing blog. December 28, 2010. <http://www.christopherakoch.com/tag/smartphones/>.

Lehmann, Donald R., and John O'Shaughnessy. "Difference in Attribute Importance for Different Industrial Products." Journal of Marketing. Vol. 38, No. 2 (Apr., 1974), pp. 36-42.

Lyon, Ethan. "How to Identify Influencers." Sparxoo Blog. July 7, 2009. <http://www.sparxoo.com/2009/07/07/how-to-identify-influencers/>.

Moran, Mike. "Scared of B2B Reviews? Get Over It." Internet Evolution.
February 9, 2009.
<http://www.internetevolution.com/author.asp?section_id=698&doc_id=171802>.

Mutimer, Sam. "Recruitment in the Social Media Age."
Australian Talent Conference social media 101 presentation. December 1, 2010.
<http://www.slideshare.net/sammutimer/sm-recruiting1>.

Noff, Ayelett. "The Top Five Reasons Brands Fear Social Media."
The Next Web blog. February 9, 2011. <http://thenextweb.com/
socialmedia/2010/02/09/top-reasons-brands-fear-social-media/>.

Ogneva, Maria. "Identifying Influencers and Measuring Influence."
The Social Customer. August 16, 2010. <http://thesocialcustomer.com/
themaria/28799/identifying-influencers-and-measuring-influence>.

Owyang, Jeremiah. "Prioritising the Coming Year: Achieve 'Escape Velocity'."
Bazaarvoice keynote presentation. October 18, 2011. <http://www.slideshare.
net/jeremiah_owyang/bazaarvoice-london-build-a-program-for-scale-keynote>.

Petouhoff, Natalie. "InfusionSoft Uses Social Media to Reduce Customer Service
Costs." Forrester.com case study. January 18, 2010. <http://blogs.forrester.com/
business_process/2010/01/case-study-3-infusionsoft-uses-social-media-to-
reduce-customer-service-costs.html>.

Pick, Tom. "The One Effective Use of Facebook for B2B Marketing."
B2B Marketing Blog. Webbiquity. March 9, 2010. <http://webbiquity.com/
social-media-marketing/the-one-effective-use-of-facebook-for-b2b-marketing/>.

Putman, Alex. "8 Ways to Engage Your LinkedIn Tribe!" Social T-Rex blog.
December 18, 2010.
<http://socialtrex.com/2010/12/18/engage-your-linkedin-tribe/>.

Ritter, Paul. "Best Practices for Using Online Video for Generating Sales Leads."
Business Video article. July 6, 2011. <http://business-video.tmcnet.com/topics/
business-video/articles/193631-part-3-best-practices-using-online-video-
generating.htm>.

Schultz, Ray. "B2B Case Study: How Kinaxis Uses Social Media."
TellAllmarketing Blog. May 20, 2010.
<http://tellallmarketing.com/blog/?p=159>.

Schulze, Holger. "B2B Content Marketing Trends."
B2B Technology Marketing Community. 2011.
<http://www.slideshare.net/hschulze/b2b-content-marketing-report>.

Schwartz, Julie, Katie Espinola and Olivier Nguyen Van Tan.
"How Customers Choose Solution Providers, 2010: The New Buyer Paradox."
ITSMA publication. January 6, 2011.

Stelzner, Michael A. Launch: How to Quickly Propel Your Business Beyond
the Competition. John Wiley & Sons, 2011.

Urlocker, Zack. "Inbound Marketing Isn't Just for Small Companies."
HubSpot Blog. March 22, 2010. <http://blog.hubspot.com/blog/tabid/6307/
bid/5754/Inbound-Marketing-Isn-t-Just-for-Small-Companies.aspx>.

Webster, Frederick E. Jr. and Yoram Wind. Organizational Buying Behavior.
Englewood Cliffs, N.J.: Prentice-Hall, 1972.

Wiegold, Keith and Joe Pulizzi. "Engagement: Understanding It, Achieving It,
Measuring It." Junta42 & Nutlug white paper. 2010.

Wilson, H. James, PJ Guinan, Salvatore Parise, and Bruce D. Weinberg.
"What's Your Social Media Strategy?" Harvard Business Review. July/August 2011.

Young, Julia. "5 Surefire Tips For Running An Effective And Engaging Webinar."
Facilitate Proceedings article. June 3, 2009. <http://facilitate.com/blog/index.
php/2009/06/5-surefire-tips-for-running-an-effective-and-engaging-webinar/>.

"B2B Marketing Tactics Not Driving Enough Sales Leads." MarketingProfs article.
March 20, 2012. <http://www.marketingprofs.com/charts/2012/7419/
b2b-marketing-tactics-not-driving-enough-sales-leads>.

"Best Practices for Organizations using Flickr."
Flickr. <http://www.flickr.com/bestpractices/>.

"Brands and Retailers Aggressively Adopt Social Media." PowerReviews.
The e-tailing group. September 16, 2009.
<http://www.e-tailing.com/content/?p=311>.

"Breaking Out Of The Funnel—A Look Inside the Mind of the New Generation
of BtoB Buyer." Genius.com/DemandGen Report white paper. 2010.

"Buzz in the Blogosphere: Millions More Bloggers and Blog Readers."
NielsenWire. March 8, 2012. <http://blog.nielsen.com/nielsenwire/online_mobile/
buzz-in-the-blogosphere-millions-more-bloggers-and-blog-readers/>.

"Cars.com Boosts Qualified Sales Leads with Bazaarvoice." Bazaarvoice.
October 20, 2008. <http://www.bazaarvoice.com/about/press-room/
carscom-boosts-qualified-sales-leads-bazaarvoice>.

"Cisco Visual Networking Index: Forecast and Methodology, 2010-2015."
Cisco white paper. June 1, 2011.

"Facebook Advertising Guidelines." Facebook.
<http://www.facebook.com/ad_guidelines.php>.

"Facebook Pages Terms." Facebook.
<http://www.facebook.com/promotions_guidelines.php>.

"Facebook's EdgeRank: How to Make Sure You're in the News Feed."
Buddy Media white paper. April 2011.

"How Customers Choose Solution Providers, 2010: The New Buyer Paradox."
ITSMA report. January 2011.

"How Vendors Can Use Remarkable Content to Attract Real Buyers."
Tippit white paper. September 2009.

"Interview and Property Releases." Copyright and Fair Use.
 Stanford University Libraries. <http://fairuse.stanford.edu/Copyright_and_Fair_
 Use_Overview/chapter12/12-d.html>.

"The annual survey of changing B2B buyer behavior."
 BuyerSphere Report 2011. Base One. 2011.

"What Your Customer Wants To Know." BrainRider presentation.
 March 2, 2011. <http://www.slideshare.net/BrainRider/
 b2b-marketing-sales-understanding-what-your-customer-wants-to-know>.

"Zero Moment of Truth – Trailer." YouTube video. Google. June 20, 2011.
 <http://www.youtube.com/watch?v=UmM9qfzfzhw>.

www.ingramcontent.com/pod-product-compliance
Lightning Source LLC
Chambersburg PA
CBHW061209220326
41599CB00025B/4577